To my wonderful wife Sandy, now with Jesus, who was a true gift from the Lord and a blessing beyond measure. She did me good, and not harm, all the days of her life.

Stephen E Atkerson
New Testament Church Dynamics: A Leader's Guide to Biblical Growth & Planting
© 2018 by New Testament Reformation Fellowship
ISBN 978-0-9729082-4-5

Special thanks to Navigation Advertising for book layout and cover design.

NTRF.org

NEW TESTAMENT
REFORMATION
FELLOWSHIP

Printed in USA

NEW TESTAMENT CHURCH DYNAMICS

A LEADER'S GUIDE TO BIBLICAL GROWTH & PLANTING

STEPHEN E. ATKERSON

CONTENTS

INTRODUCTION

In His Great Commission, Jesus said to make disciples of all nations, teaching them to observe all He commanded.[1] Thus, we see that healthy church growth is both numerical and spiritual. Evangelism and disciple-making should be inextricably bound.

One New Testament growth dynamic is ever increasing love. Jesus taught, "love one another: just as I have loved you."[2] Yet love is also a shrewd evangelistic method. Jesus went on to declare that "all people will know that you are my disciples, if you have love for one another."[3]

Another dynamic of healthy growth is found in a church's unity. Jesus prayed that "they may all be one, just as you, Father, are in me, and I in you, that they also may be in us, so that the world may believe that you have sent me."[4] Did you notice how oneness, like love, also plays a role in furthering our witness?

How can we increase love and unity in our churches, which, in turn, aids in our witness to the world? Looking to the Scriptures, we find that the various practices of the first-century church were carefully designed by the Apostles to honor Christ, foster love, create oneness and promote active engagement in the life of the congregation. These practices, in turn, supernaturally result in a positive witness and more evangelism. There are four critical—yet neglected—early church dynamics that still have great potential to grow love and unity in churches today.

Believers involved in churches that follow these four practices have testified how they enjoyed fellowship in a way never before experienced. Deep appreciation has also been expressed for congregational participation during the time of worship, for the many opportunities for each member to minister using his spiritual gifts, for the emphasis on mutual encouragement and

---

[1]Matthew 28:19-20.
[2]John 13:34.
[3]John 13:35.
[4]John 17:21.

1

for servant leadership that is not lording over people (but is instead building congregational consensus).[5] Couple all these benefits with intentional disciple-making through strong biblical teaching and the stage is set for significant growth in the Lord and a meaningful church experience.

The chapters that follow are the result of years of research into the ways of the apostles combined with over twenty-five years of experience with churches that have incorporated these practices. Each of the four practices has a chapter laying out its scriptural basis and benefit plus an appendix with practical considerations for implementation. May the Lord be pleased to use these truths to build up His Church.

---

[5] Comments repeatedly made to the author in over twenty-five years of being involved with such churches.

1

THE LORD'S SUPPER– A FELLOWSHIP FEAST

How could early church practice enrich your Lord's Supper observances? *Consider making a weekly Agapé meal an integral part of it.* The first-century church celebrated the Lord's Supper weekly in conjunction with the Love Feast. This holy meal was a wonderful time of both unification and fellowship. It was also a vivid reminder of Jesus' promise to come back and eat it again with us.

PROFIT

The elements of communion look back to Jesus' death on the cross to pay for sin. The *Agapé* adds a forward look. When celebrated as a feast in a joyful wedding atmosphere, the Lord's Supper typifies the wedding supper of the Lamb. It is a regular reminder of Jesus' promise to return and eat it with us. A major benefit of celebrating the Lord's Supper as a holy banquet is the fellowship and encouragement experienced by each member of Christ's body. This relaxed, unhurried fellowship meal with God's family is a significant means of edifying the Church, building community, cementing ties of love, and supernaturally creating unity.

PROOF

The setting of the first Lord's Supper was the Passover Feast. Jesus and His disciples reclined around a table abundant with food (Ex 12, De 16). During the course of the meal ("*while they were eating,*" Mt 26:26), Jesus took a loaf and compared it to his body. Then, "*after* the supper" (Lk 22:20), He took the cup and compared it to his blood, soon to be poured out for sin. Timing is everything. The bread and wine of the Lord's

Supper were introduced in the context of an actual meal. As with Passover, the Twelve would have understood the bread and wine of the Lord's Supper to also be part of an actual meal. The Greek for "supper", *deipnon*, means dinner or banquet, the main meal toward evening.[1] It arguably never refers to anything less than a full meal. That the authors of the New Testament chose *deipnon* to refer to the Lord's "Supper" suggests they understood it to be a full meal.

At the Last Supper, Jesus said, "I confer on you a kingdom...so that you may eat and drink at my table in my kingdom" (Lk 22:29-30). Why eschatological eating? First-century Jews thought of heaven as a time of feasting at Messiah's table. For instance, a Jewish leader once said to Jesus, "Blessed is everyone who will eat bread in the kingdom of God!" (Lk 14:15). Jesus Himself spoke of those who will "take their places at the feast with Abraham, Isaac and Jacob in the kingdom of heaven" (Mt 8:11).[2]

Isaiah described the coming kingdom feast in this way: "the LORD of hosts will make for all peoples a feast of rich food, a feast of well-aged wine, of rich food full of marrow, of aged wine well refined ... He will swallow up death forever; and the Lord GOD will wipe away tears from all faces, and the reproach of his people he will take away from all the earth, for the LORD has spoken" (Isa 25:6-8). The book of Revelation describes a future time of feasting at the wedding banquet of the Lamb (Re 19:9).

The early church observed the Lord's Supper as a true meal along with the bread and cup. It is important to appreciate why the Lord's Supper was originally an actual meal. It is a picture and foretaste of what we will be doing when Jesus returns to eat it again with us. What better way to typify the marriage banquet of the Lamb than with a meal manifesting all of the excitement, fellowship, and love that the heavenly banquet will have?

---

[1] Bauer, Arndt, Gingrich, Danker, *A Greek-English Lexicon of the New Testament* (Chicago, IL: University of Chicago Press, 1979) 173; (used in 1 Corinthians 11:20).
[2] This picture of heaven as dining in God's presence may have originated in the Sinai experience. The elders of Israel went with Moses to the top of the mountain. Moses noted that "God did not raise his hand against these leaders of the Israelites." Instead, "they saw God, and they ate and drank" (Ex 24:11).

The most extensive treatment of the Lord's Supper is found in 1 Corinthians 10-11. The church in Corinth clearly celebrated it as an actual meal. However, class and cultural divisions resulted in their communion meetings doing more harm than good (11:17-18). The upper class, not wanting to dine with those of a lower social class, evidently came to the gathering early to avoid the poor. By the time the working class believers arrived, delayed perhaps by employment constraints, all the food had been eaten. The poor went home hungry (11:21-22). The wealthy failed to esteem their impoverished brethren as equal members of the body of Christ (11:23-32).

The Corinthian abuse was so serious that what was supposed to be the *Lord's* Supper had instead become their *own* supper: "When you come together, it is not the Lord's supper that you eat. For in eating, each one goes ahead with his own meal" (11:20-21). If merely eating one's own supper were the entire objective, then private dining at home would be sufficient. Thus Paul asked the rich, "Do you not have houses to eat and drink in?" (11:22). However, from the nature of the abuse, it is evident that the Corinthian church regularly partook of the Lord's Supper as a full meal.

It has been suggested that abuses in Corinth led Paul to put an end to the meal. For instance, the original commentary in the *Geneva Bible* of 1599 states, "The Apostle thinketh it good to take away the love feasts, for their abuse, although they had been a long time, and with commendation used in Churches, and were appointed and instituted by the Apostles."[3] To this we wonder, would Paul single-handedly overturn something established by Jesus Himself, taught by the other apostles and practiced in all the churches? Though in humble disagreement with those who penned the commentary, their acknowledgment that the Lord's Supper and the love feast were celebrated together and instituted by the apostles is appreciated.

It has been said that the best antidote to abuse is not disuse, but proper use. Paul's solution to Corinthian abuse was *not* to do away with the meal. Instead, Paul wrote, "when you

---

[3] *1599 Geneva Bible* (White Hall, WV: Tolle Lege Press, 2006), 1180.

come together to eat, wait for each other" (11:33). Only those so famished they could not wait for the others are instructed to "eat at home" (1Co 11:34). Commentator C.K. Barrett cautioned, "Paul's point is that, if the rich wish to eat and drink on their own, enjoying better food than their poorer brothers, they should do this at home; if they cannot wait for others (verse 33), if they must indulge to excess, they can at least keep the church's common meal free from practices that can only bring discredit upon it ... Paul simply means that those who are so hungry that they cannot wait for their brothers should satisfy their hunger before they leave home, in order that decency and order may prevail in the assembly."[4]

In summary, it is clear from Scripture that, in the early church, the bread and wine of the Lord's Supper were partaken of in the context of a holy feast. Communion was not only with the Lord through the elements but also with each other through the meal. This early church practice builds community and unity, edifies the church, and typifies the coming eschatological feast. Celebrating the Lord's Supper as an actual meal is like the rehearsal dinner for a great wedding feast the next day.

PROFESSORS

The opinion of scholars is clearly weighted toward the conclusion that the Lord's Supper was originally eaten as a full meal. For example, in his massive work *New Testament Theology*, Donald Guthrie stated that the apostle Paul "sets the Lord's supper in the context of the fellowship meal."[5] Gordon Fee, editor of the notable evangelical commentary series, the *New International Commentary on the New Testament*, pointed out "the nearly universal phenomenon of cultic meals as a part of worship in antiquity" and "the fact that in the early church the Lord's Supper was most likely eaten as, or in conjunction with, such a meal." Fee further noted that, "from the beginning the *Last* Supper was for Christians not

---

[4]C. K. Barrett, The Fist Epistle to The Corinthians, *Black's New Testament Commentary*, (Peabody, MA: Hendrickson Publishers, 1968), 263 & 277.
[5]Donald Guthrie, *New Testament Theology* (Downers Grove, IL: Inter-Varsity Press, 1981), 758.

an annual Christian Passover, but a regularly repeated meal in 'honor of the Lord,' hence the *Lord's* Supper."[6]

G. W. Grogan, writing for the *New Bible Dictionary*, observed, "the administration of the Eucharist shows it set in the context of a fellowship supper ... The separation of the meal or Agape from the Eucharist lies outside the times of the NT."[7] In his commentary on 1 Corinthians, C. K. Barrett made the observation that "the Lord's Supper was still at Corinth an ordinary meal to which acts of symbolical significance were attached, rather than a purely symbolical meal."[8]

According to Dr. John Gooch, editor at the United Methodist Publishing House, "In the first century, the Lord's Supper included not only the bread and the cup but an entire meal."[9] Yale professor J.J. Pelikan concluded, "often, if not always, it [the Lord's Supper] was celebrated in the setting of a common meal."[10]

PERSPECTIVE: A FUTURE FOCUS

According to Fritz Reinecker, "The Passover celebrated two events, the deliverance from Egypt and the anticipated coming Messianic deliverance."[11] It had both backward and forward-looking aspects. When Jesus turned the Passover Feast into the Lord's Supper, He also gave it both backward and forward-looking aspects. It looks back to Jesus' sacrifice as the ultimate Passover Lamb, delivering His people from their sins. It looks forward to the time Jesus will come and eat it again with us. The *Baptist Faith and Message* of 2000 says, "The Lord's Supper is a symbolic act of obedience whereby

[6]Gordon Fee, *The First Epistle to The Corinthians*, New International Commentary on the New Testament, (Grand Rapids, MI: Wm. B. Eerdmans Publishing Co., 1987), 532 & 555.

[7]G. W. Grogan, "Love Feast," *The New Bible Dictionary*, ed. J. D. Douglas, (Wheaton, IL: Tyndale House Publishers, 1982), 712.

[8]C. K. Barrett, The Fist Epistle to The Corinthians, *Black's New Testament Commentary*, (Peabody, MA: Hendrickson Publishers, 1968), 276.

[9]John Gooch, *Christian History & Biography*, Issue 37 (Carol Stream, IL: Christianity Today) p. 3.

[10]Jaroslav Pelikan, "Eucharist," *Encyclopaedia Britannica*, ed. Warren Preece, Vol. 8 (Chicago: William Benton, Publisher, 1973), 808.

[11]Fritz Reinecker & Cleon Rogers, *Linguistic Key to the Greek New Testament* (Grand Rapids, MI: Zondervan, 1980), 207.

members of the church, through partaking of the bread and the fruit of the vine, memorialize the death of the Redeemer and *anticipate His second coming*" (italics mine).[12]

R.P. Martin, Professor of New Testament at Fuller Theological Seminary, wrote that there are "eschatological overtones" to the Lord's Supper "with a forward look to the advent in glory."[13] The future kingdom of God was much on the Lord's mind during the Last Supper. Jesus first mentioned the future at the beginning of the Passover: "I will not eat it until it is fulfilled in the kingdom of God" (Lk 22:16). "Until" (*heos houtou*) is a forward-looking word. Jesus' use of the word "fulfilled" suggests there is something prophetic about it.

Jesus mentioned the future a second time when passing the cup: "from now on I will not drink of the fruit of the vine until the kingdom of God comes" (Lk 22:18). Every time we partake of the cup, Jesus' promise to return and drink it again with us at the wedding banquet of the Lamb should be brought to mind. After the supper He referred to the future a third time, saying, "I confer on you a kingdom ... so that you may eat and drink at my table in my kingdom" (Lk 22:29-30).

Thus, we see that Jesus gave the Lord's Supper numerous forward-looking aspects. As a full meal, it prefigures the marriage supper of the Lamb. When we partake of the cup we should be reminded of His words, "I will not drink of the fruit of the vine until the kingdom of God comes" (Lk 22:18). The *Encyclopaedia Britannica* declared that "early Christianity regarded this institution as a mandate ... learning to know, even in this present life, the joys of the heavenly banquet that was to come in the kingdom of God ... the past, the present, and the future came together in the Eucharist."[14]

1 Corinthians 11:26 states that through the Lord's Supper we proclaim the Lord's death "until" He comes. The word "until" normally denotes a time frame. For example, an

---

[12]"The Baptist Faith and Message", sbc.net, accessed September 6, 2016.
[13]R. P. Martin, "The Lord's Supper," *The New Bible Dictionary*, ed. J. D. Douglas (Wheaton, IL: Tyndale House Publishers, 1982), 709.
[14]Pelikan, 808.

umbrella is used *until* it stops raining. Then it is put away. Using the umbrella does not cause the rain to stop. In this case, however, Paul's statement has more to do with why we proclaim it. The Greek behind "until" is unusual (*achri hou*). Conservative German theology professor Fritz Rienecker pointed out that as it is used here (with an aorist subjunctive verb), it denotes much more than a mere time frame; grammatically it can denote a goal or an objective.[15]

In *The Eucharistic Words of Jesus*, it is argued that the Greek underlying "until" (*achri hou*, 1Co 11:26) is not simply a temporal reference, but functions as a kind of final clause. That is, the meal's function is as a constant reminder to God to bring about the Second Coming.[16] Paul was instructing the church to partake of the bread and cup as a means of proclaiming the Lord's death with the goal of His return. Thus, in proclaiming His death through the loaf and cup, the Supper looked forward to and anticipated His return.

According to Professor Herman Ridderbos, "It is not merely a subjective recalling to mind, but an active manifestation of the continuing and actual significance of the death of Christ. 'Proclaim' in this respect has a prophetic, declaratory significance ... Everything is directed not only toward the past, but also toward the future. It is the proclamation that in the death of Christ the new and eternal covenant of grace has taken effect, if still in a provisional and not yet consummated sense."[17]

It is interesting that the earliest believers, in *Didache* x. 6, used *maran atha* ("Our Lord, come") as a prayer in connection with the Lord's Supper, "a context at once eucharistic and eschatological."[18] Linking this back to the situation in Corinth, Dr. R. P. Martin writes, "*Maranatha* in 1 Cor. 16:22 may very well be placed in a eucharistic setting so that the conclusion of the letter ends with the invocation 'Our Lord, come!' and

---

[15]Reinecker, 427. Other instances of this construction in eschatological passages include Luke 21:24, Romans 11:25 and 1 Corinthians 15:25.

[16]Joachim Jeremias, *The Eucharistic Words of Jesus* (New York, NY: Charles Scribner's Sons, 1966), 252-254.

[17]Herman Ridderbos, *Paul: An Outline of His Theology*, translated by John R. deWitt (Grand Rapids: Eerdmans, 1975), 422.

[18]Barrett, 397.

prepares the scene for the celebration of the meal after the letter has been read to the congregation."[19]

PURPOSE # 1—FELLOWSHIP

In ancient Jewish thought, eating with someone symbolized acceptance and fellowship. Thus, in Revelation 3:20, Jesus offered to "eat" (*deipneo*) with anyone who heard His voice and opened the door. One of the major blessings of celebrating the Lord's Supper as an actual feast is the genuine fellowship everyone enjoys. This fellowship in feasting theme is evident in the book of Acts. A casual reading of Acts 2:42 suggests the Church was devoted to four things: the apostles teaching, fellowship, the breaking of bread, and prayer. However, a closer examination reveals there were only three things to which they were devoted: teaching, fellowship in the breaking of bread, and prayer. (In Greek the words "fellowship" and "breaking of bread" are linked together as simultaneous activities.)[20] It was F.F. Bruce's position that the fellowship of Acts 2:42 was expressed practically in the breaking of bread.[21] They had fellowship with one another *as* they broke bread together. Luke further informs us that this eating was done with "glad and sincere hearts" (2:46). Sounds inviting, doesn't it?

Many churches observe the Lord's Supper with a funeral atmosphere. An organ softly plays reflective music. Every head is bowed and every eye closed as people quietly and introspectively search their souls for sin needing confession. Down front, the elements are laid out on a rectangular table, covered with a white cloth, almost like a casket at a funeral. Somber deacons, like pallbearers, distribute the elements. Dutch theologian Karl Deddens noticed that "Under the influence of pietism and mysticism, a sense of 'unworthiness' is awakened within them, and

---

[19]Martin, 709.

[20]In many English versions there is an "and" between "teaching" and "fellowship," then between "bread" and "prayer," but not between "fellowship" and "bread" (Ac 2:42). This is because, in some Greek manuscripts, the words "fellowship" and "breaking of bread" are linked together as simultaneous activities (no *kai* between fellowship and the breaking of bread).

[21]F. F. Bruce, *Acts of The Apostles* (Grand Rapids, MI: Wm. B. Eerdmans Publishing Co., 1981) 79.

they become afraid that they may be 'eating and drinking judgment unto themselves.' As for those who were still bold enough to go to the table of the Lord, their faces suggest that a funeral is under way rather than a celebration."[22] Is this really in keeping with the tradition of the apostles concerning the Supper?

It was the unworthy *manner* that Paul criticized (1Co 11:27), not the unworthy *people*. The unworthy manner consisted of drunkenness at the table of the Lord, of not eating together, and of causing the poor to go home hungry and humiliated. This failure of the rich to recognize the body of the Lord in their poorer brethren resulted in divine judgment: many of them were sick, and a number had even died (1Co 11:27-32). Indeed, every person ought to examine himself before arriving to be sure he is not guilty of the same gross sin—failing to recognize the body of the Lord in one's fellow believers (1Co 11:28-29). Once we have each judged ourselves, we can come to the meal without fear of judgment and enjoy the fellowship of the Lord's Supper as the true wedding banquet it is intended to be.

Commentators often associate the Lord's Supper with the phrase "breaking of bread" throughout the book of Acts. This is because Luke, who wrote Acts, recorded in his gospel that Jesus took bread and broke it at the last supper (Lk 22:19). F.F. Bruce held that the phrase "breaking of bread" denotes "something more than the ordinary partaking of food together: the regular observance of the Lord's Supper is no doubt indicated ... this observance appears to have formed the part of an ordinary meal."[23] If this conclusion is accurate, it means the early church enjoyed the Lord's Supper as a time of fellowship and gladness, just like one would enjoy at a wedding banquet: "breaking bread in their homes, they received their food with glad and generous hearts, praising God and having favor with all the people" (Acts 2:46-47).

---

[22]Karl Deddens, *Where Everything Points to Him*, translated by Theodore Plantinga (Neerlandia, AB: Inheritance Publications, 1993), 93.

[23]Bruce, 79.

A middle-aged man, new in Christ and to church, sat through a number of traditional Sunday services. Finally he said, "I see people greet each other just before the service. As soon as it ends they hug good-bye and quickly head home. I'm not getting to know anyone. What is the Christian equivalent of the neighborhood bar?"[24] Celebrating the Lord's Supper weekly as a relaxed fellowship meal is the biblical answer to his question. We all desire church relationships that are genuine and meaningful, not just a friendly church but a church where our friends are with us. The Lord's Supper can help make this a reality.

To get the most out of the fellowship aspect of the holy meal, it should be celebrated often. Early believers ate the Lord's Supper weekly as one of the main purposes for their coming together as a church every Lord's Day. The *Encyclopaedia Britannica* judged the Lord's Supper to be "the central rite of Christian worship" and "has been an indispensable component of the Christian service since the earliest days of the church."[25]

The first evidence of weekly communion is grammatical. To Christians, Sunday is the "Lord's Day" (Re 1:10), the day Jesus rose from the dead. This translates unique technical wording in Greek (*kuriakon hemeran*). It is literally "the day belonging to the Lord." The words "belonging to the Lord" are from *kuriakos*, found in the New Testament only in Revelation 1:10 and in 1 Corinthians 11:20, where it to refers to the Supper "belonging to the Lord" (*kuriakon deipnon*). The connection between these two identical and unusual grammatical uses must not be missed. The *supper* belonging to the Lord was eaten every week on the *day* belonging to the Lord. The Lord's Day, and the Lord's Supper go together as a package deal once a week.

More evidence for the weekly celebration of the Lord's Supper is found in the only clear reason ever given in Scripture for the regular purpose of a church meeting: To eat the Lord's Supper. In Acts 20:7, Luke informs, "On the first day of the

---

[24]Conversation with the author, mid-1980s.
[25]Pelikan, 807.

12

week we came together to break bread." The words "to break bread" in Acts 20:7 are known as a telic infinitive denoting a purpose or objective. They met in order to break bread.

Another place where the New Testament states the purpose for a church gathering is 1 Corinthians 11:17-22. Their "meetings" (11:17) were doing more harm than good because when they came "together as a church" (11:18a) they had deep division. Thus, Paul wrote, "when you come together, it is not the Lord's Supper you eat" (11:20). From this, it is obvious the reason for their weekly church meetings ostensibly was to eat the Lord's Supper.

The third and last reference to the explicitly stated reason for an assembly is found in 1 Corinthians 11:33, "When you come together *to eat*, wait for each other" (italics mine). As before, it states the reason they came together was to eat. Lest this appear to be making much out of little, it must be realized that no other reason is ever given in the Scriptures as to the purpose of a regular, weekly church meeting. It is obvious from Scripture that they also had times of worship and teaching each Sunday, but the driving focus of the gathering was communion.

Several early extra-biblical sources indicate the church celebrated the Lord's Supper weekly. One is Justin Martyr's *First Apology*, written in the middle of the second century. Another is the *Didache*. Around A.D. 200, Hippolytus wrote of a typical worship service in Rome, which included the Lord's Supper. The New Testament church practice of celebrating the Holy Meal weekly continues on in both Orthodoxy and Catholicism. Protestant thinker John Calvin also advocated weekly communion.[26]

Dutch Reformed theologian Dr. K. Deddens wrote, "If the Lord's Supper were celebrated more often, we should not view such a change as an accommodation to 'sacramentalists' who wish to place less emphasis on the service of the Word; rather, we should view it as an execution of Christ's command ..."[27] The fellowship and

---

[26]David Koyzis, "The Lord's Supper: How Often?", www.reformedworship.org, accessed September 1, 2016.
[27]Deddens, 93.

encouragement that each member enjoys in such a weekly gathering is tremendous. This aspect of the Church's Sunday meeting should not be rushed or replaced. It is also important to be devoted to the apostle's teaching and prayer, but not at the expense of the weekly Lord's Supper. Celebrating the Holy Meal weekly adds a dynamic to church meetings that cannot be equaled.

PURPOSE #2—UNITY

Celebrating the Lord's Supper each week as a fellowship meal goes a long way in building unity. Also important is the visible presentation of the elements. Mention is made in Scripture of *the* cup of thanksgiving (a single cup, 1Co 10:16) and of only *one* loaf: "Because there is one loaf, we, who are many, are one body, for we all partake of the one loaf" (1Co 10:17).[28] Using one cup and one loaf pictures our oneness in Christ. The imagery presented by broken cracker crumbs and multiple cups is that of disunity, division, and individuality.

The one loaf not only pictures our unity in Christ but, according to 1 Corinthians 10:17, partaking of it may even create unity! Notice carefully the wording of the inspired text. "Because" there is one loaf, therefore we are one body, "for" we all partake of the one loaf (1Co 10:17). One scholar wrote that the Lord's Supper was "intended as means of fostering the unity of the church ... "[29] Professor Gerd Theissen said, "Because all have eaten portions of the same element, they have become a unity in which they have come as close to one another as members of the same body, as if the bodily boundaries between and among people had been transcended."[30] In their commentary on Corinthians, Robertson and Plummer concluded, "The single loaf is a symbol and an instrument of unity."[31] Gordon

---

[28]NIV.

[29]Jaroslav Jan Pelikan, "Eucharist," *Encyclopaedia Britannica*, ed. Warren Preece, Vol. 8 (Chicago: William Benton Publisher, 1973), 807.

[30]Gerd Theissen, *The Social Setting of Pauline Christianity: Essays on Corinth* (Eugene, OR: Wipf & Stock Publishers, 1982), 165.

[31]Robertson & Plummer, The International Critical Commentary on the Holy Scriptures of the Old and New Testaments, 1 Corinthians (New York: Charles Scribner's Sons, 1911), 213.

Fee wrote of the "solidarity of the fellowship of believers created by their all sharing 'the one loaf.' "[32]

Some in Corinth were guilty of taking the Lord's Supper in an unworthy manner (1Co 11:27). Shameful class divisions cut at the heart of the unity the Lord's Supper is designed to symbolize. What was Paul's solution to the harmful meetings? "So then, my brothers, when you come together to eat, wait for each other" (1Co 11:33). Part of the reason the Corinthians were not unified is precisely because they failed to eat the Lord's Supper *together*, as an actual meal, centered around the one cup and one loaf.

In the Lord's Supper we practically express our oneness in Christ. Jesus prayed "that they may be one even as we are one." This fundamental practice reflects the big eternal picture of the Church and Christianity: "There is one body and one Spirit—just as you were called to the one hope that belongs to your call—one Lord, one faith, one baptism, one God and Father of all, who is over all and through all and in all" (Ep 4:4-6). Our unity together in Christ is a powerful witness. Jesus prayed that we "may all be one ... so that the world may believe that you have sent me."[33]

PURPOSE #3—A REMINDER

In the covenant God made with Noah, He promised never to again destroy the earth by flood. What is the purpose of the rainbow? God declared, "whenever the rainbow appears in the clouds, *I* will see it and *remember* the everlasting covenant between God and all living creatures" (Ge 9:16, italics mine). Wayne Grudem has pointed out how the Bible "frequently speaks of God 'remembering' something and therefore I do not think it inappropriate or inconsistent for us to speak this way when we want to refer to God's awareness of events that have happened in our past, events he recognizes as already having occurred

---

[32] Gordon Fee, *The New International Commentary On The New Testament, 1 Corinthians* (Grand Rapids: Wm. B Eerdman's, 2014), 515.
[33] John 17:21.

and therefore as being 'past.' "[34] It is a biblical fact that God remembers covenant promises.

In His covenant with Abraham, God promised to bring the Israelites out of Egyptian bondage. Accordingly, at the appointed time, "God heard their groaning, and *God remembered* his covenant with Abraham" (Ex 2:24, italics mine). God remembers covenant promises.

During the Babylonian captivity, God promised the Jews, "*I* will *remember* my covenant with you" (the Sinai covenant; Eze 16:60, italics mine). God remembers covenant promises.

In the Lord's Supper the fruit of the vine represents the "blood of the covenant" (Mt 26:28). The bread symbolizes Jesus body. Jesus said to partake of the bread "in remembrance of Me" (Lk 22:19). The bread and wine bring to our remembrance Jesus' body and blood given for us.

The Greek for "remembrance," *anamnesis*, fundamentally means "reminder." A reminder can remind about something that already happened in the past or that is supposed to happen in the future. Translating *ananmesis* as "remembrance" leads us to think only of Jesus' past sacrifice on the cross. However, if *anamnesis* is translated more simply as "reminder", it could be understood to refer to the something in the past (Jesus' death on the cross) and in the future (Jesus' promise to return).

As we have already seen, God also remembers covenant promises. Another very significant function of the Lord's Supper may be as a reminder to Jesus Himself of His covenant promise to return.[35] Jesus literally said, "do this unto my reminder." The word "my" in "my reminder" translates the Greek *emou*. More than a mere personal pronoun, it is a possessive pronoun. This suggests the reminder is not simply about Jesus, it actually belongs to Jesus. It is His reminder. Lutheran theologian Joachim Jeremias understood Jesus to use *anamnesis* in the sense of

---

[34]Wayne Grudem, "The Nature of Divine Eternity, A Response to William Craig," WayneGrudem.com, accessed September 03, 2016.

[35]Statements about God remembering or being reminded are, of course, anthropomorphic. An omniscient God neither forgets nor needs reminding.

a reminder for God, "The Lord's Supper would thus be an enacted prayer."[36] Just as seeing the rainbow reminds God of His covenant promise never to flood the world again, so too when Jesus sees us partake of the Lord's Supper it reminds Him of His promise to return and eat it again with us. Understood in this light, it is designed to be like a prayer asking Jesus to return ("Thy kingdom come," Lk 11:2). God remembers covenant promises.

In summary, when we partake of the bread and wine, we are reminded of Jesus' body and blood, given for the remission of sin. Along with Jesus, we should also be reminded of His promise to come back and eat it again with us. Celebrating the Lord's Supper is an acted out prayer for Jesus to return. *Maranatha!*

PROPOSITION

As was demonstrated above, there is general agreement within the scholarly circles that the early church celebrated the Lord's Supper as a genuine meal. However, the post-apostolic church has had no use for this practice. According to Dr. Williston Walker, a well-respected professor of church history at Yale, "by the time Justin Martyr wrote his *Apology* in Rome (153), the common meal had disappeared, and the Supper was joined with the assembly for preaching, as a concluding sacrament."[37]

The church of history has, at various points and for a time, deviated from New Testament patterns. For instance, credo baptism was essentially unheard of within Christendom for well over a millennia. Yet, since the time of the Reformation, this long neglected apostolic tradition is again widely practiced. Another example can be found in the separation of church and state, a New Testament example that was disregarded in European church history as the sword of the state was welded to the cross. Today, however, most believers again hold to the separation of the two. The church may be missing a tremendous blessing in neglecting the practice of

---

[36]Colin Brown, *New International Dictionary of New Testament Theology*, Vol. III (Grand Rapids, MI: Zondervan, 1981) 244.
[37]Walker, 38.

the early church regarding the Lord's Supper. Proposition: as this was the practice of the early church, should we not follow their example?

- The Lord's Supper was the primary purpose for which the New Testament church gathered each Lord's Day.

- It was celebrated as a feast, in a joyful, wedding atmosphere rather than in a somber, funeral atmosphere.

- A major benefit of the Supper as a banquet is the fellowship and encouragement each member experiences.

- Eaten as a banquet, the Supper typifies the marriage supper of the Lamb and has a forward-looking component.

- Within the context of this full meal, there is to be one cup and one loaf to both symbolize and even create unity in a body of believers.

- The bread and wine symbolize Jesus' body and blood. They also serve as reminders of Jesus' promise to return and eat it again us (Amen. Come quickly, Lord Jesus!).

DISCUSSION QUESTIONS

1. What is the scholarly consensus as to how the early church celebrated the Lord's Supper? Why does this consensus matter?

2. How was the original focus of the Lord's Supper both past-looking and forward-looking?

3. If Acts 2:42-47 refers to the Lord's Supper, how would you describe their mood?

4. What theological reason did Paul give for using a single loaf in the Lord's Supper?

5. What indicators are there in 1 Corinthians 11:17-22 that the Lord's Supper was eaten as an actual meal?

6. Why does the word "until" in 1 Corinthians 11:26 indicate purpose and not merely duration?

7. What "unworthy manner" made some in Corinth guilty of sinning against the body and blood of the Lord (1Co 11:27)? How should this impact us today?

8. What, in 1 Corinthians 11:33-34, was the inspired solution to abuse of the Lord's Supper?

9. What is the only reason ever given in the New Testament as to why the early church came together each Lord's Day?

10. What blessings might a church miss by not celebrating the Lord's Supper as an actual holy meal?

For practical issues related to celebrating the Lord' Supper as a holy meal see Appendix A.

Audio and video presentations on communion, along with a teacher's discussion guide, can be accessed at NTRF.org.

2

PARTICIPATORY WORSHIP – UNLEASHING THE LAITY

How could early church practice make your worship services more meaningful? *Consider unleashing the laity.* Ordinary believers regularly and significantly contributed to the corporate worship of the first-century church. This open format allowed those prompted by the Spirit to offer testimony, share a spiritual experience, give an exhortation, lead out in prayer, testify, sing, give praises, etc. In general, each person who spoke operated out of his spiritual gifting. According to Scripture, the prime directive for anything said or done was that it had to edify (strengthen, build up, encourage) all the other believers present.[1]

PROFIT

A major profit of participatory worship is in allowing for a fuller expression of the spiritual gifts that involve speaking. It is in keeping with the principle of the various "one another" passages of Scripture.[2] It gets people more involved in church meetings. Congregational interest is heightened, as the proceedings of the meeting can be contributed to in a truly meaningful way. Furthermore, since the things shared come directly from the congregation, they tend to be practical, from the heart, and drawn from the application of God's Word to everyday life situations.

PROOF

What scriptural proof is there that New Testament church worship was participatory?

---

[1] "Let all things be done for building up" (1Co 14:26).
[2] There are 59 "one another" passages, such as John 13:34, Romans 12:10, 1 Peter 4:8, 1 John 3:11, 23, 4:7, etc.

Open Synagogue Format: Even though he was a stranger to them, Paul was able to preach the Gospel in synagogues throughout the Roman world because first-century synagogues were open to participation from those in attendance.[3] Had ancient synagogue meetings been anything like most modern worship services, Paul would have had to find another way to reach the Jews with the gospel! As Jewish Christians comprised the first churches, it is no wonder the meetings of these Jewish believers were also open to audience input.[4]

Encourage One Another: Early believers were responsible for thinking carefully how each could spur others on when they met together as a church. Thus, the author of Hebrews urged ordinary Christians to "consider how to stir up one another to love and good works, not neglecting to meet together ... but encouraging one another."[5] Watchman Nee pointed out that all members of Christ's body bear equal responsibility to encourage one another. Worship was formatted in such a way to allow ample opportunity for mutual encouragement. The focus was not exclusively on leaders. It was about each member doing his part as led by the Spirit.[6]

Each One Has: 1 Corinthians 14 regulates the use of multiple verbal spiritual gifts in church gatherings. In describing their meetings, Paul wrote, "What then, brothers? When you come together, each one has a hymn, a lesson, a revelation, a tongue, or an interpretation."[7] Those brothers with verbal spiritual gifts used them in the gathering to build up the church. New Testament believers did not merely *attend* services. They were active, vital participants who could significantly contribute to what went on in the gathering.[8] Their motto for church meetings could have been "Every member a

---

[3]Acts 13:14-15, 14:1, 17:1-2, 17:10, 18:4, 19:8.

[4]We do not advocate incorporating Jewish synagogue practices in church. The point is simply to show how participatory worship was not an unfamiliar idea to the earliest Christians.

[5]Hebrews 10:24-25.

[6]The Spirit's prompting is an essential element in participatory worship. Otherwise, it would merely be a religious version of the amateur hour. Every believer has been given a spiritual gift to be used to build up the church and is to operate out of this gifting. It is leadership's duty to equip the church to understand and practice this.

[7]1 Corinthians 14:26.

[8]Not every person should be expected to say something at every gathering.

minister." There was lively audience participation.[9] (See Appendix A for practical examples of this).

Edification: 1 Corinthians 14 deals with the regulation of participatory worship when "the whole church comes together."[10] The over-arching purpose for anything said or done in such a gathering is that it must edify the church: "Let all things be done for building up" (1Co 14:26). The Greek for building up (*oikodomé*) means strengthening or edifying. One lexicon described *oikodomé* as the action of one who promotes another's growth in Christian wisdom, piety, and holiness.[11] Any comment made in participatory worship was driven by the Spirit and lovingly designed to encourage, build up, strengthen or edify the other believers present. If not, it was inappropriate and was to be left unspoken. Every testimony had to be thought out so as to build up the church. To be edifying, all teaching had to be both true and application-oriented. Any music had to honor the Lord and be theologically sound. Those who prophesied spoke to others for "upbuilding and encouragement and consolation" (1Co 14:3). [12] The Corinthians were told, "since you are eager for manifestations of the Spirit, strive to excel in building up the church" (1Co 14:12). All this points to the participatory nature of early church gatherings as each person ministered according to his oral spiritual gift.

Music: 1 Corinthians 14 is about the regulation of spiritual gifts in worship. Paul wrote that "each one" had the opportunity to bring a "hymn" (14:26). He likely meant each one gifted in music. Any Spirit-led musician in good standing with the church had the freedom to edify the congregation through his gift. Those gifted in music also facilitate the entire church's singing in worship. It was the elders' duty to be sure all music was edifying (theologically accurate, easy for the average person to sing, and beautiful).

---

[9]1 Corinthians 14:33b-35 apparently limits the participation to men. See Appendix A for more on this.

[10]1 Corinthians 14:23.

[11]Joseph Thayer, *Greek-English Lexicon of the New Testament* (Grand Rapids, MI: Baker Book House, 1977), 40.

[12]Even convicting reproofs can be edifying.

Even the early church's singing had a "one another" emphasis, with believers "addressing one another in psalms and hymns and spiritual songs, singing and making melody to the Lord with all your heart."[13] It appears that believers in the early church generally had the freedom to request or introduce songs. Colossian Christians were exhorted to be "admonishing one another with psalms and hymns and spiritual songs, singing with thankfulness in your hearts to God."[14]

Paul Talked with Them: Acts 20:7 records that Paul, when visiting Troas, spoke until midnight. The Greek verb describing what he did is *dialegomai*. Our word "dialogue" is transliterated from it. It primarily means discuss.[15] Thus, the ESV states that Paul "talked with" them. In Acts 18:4 and 19:8, the same word is rendered as "reasoned" and "reasoning". Paul undoubtedly did most of the speaking that night, but the way he taught was not via an uninterrupted sermon, as if broadcasting over the radio. Thus, we see the early church's teaching times, even those led by an apostle, were to some degree discussion oriented, another indicator church meetings were participatory.[16]

Lessons: In-depth biblical exposition that was application-oriented was an integral part of each weekly church meeting. Taking disciple-making seriously means teaching all that Jesus commanded. Although elders rightly do most of the teaching on the Lord's Day, in New Testament days "each one" of the brothers who had the gift of teaching also had the freedom to bring the weekly "lesson" (1Co 14:26).[17] There clearly was an opportunity for supernaturally gifted and mature brothers active in the fellowship to teach (with the elders' approval and coaching).[18] James' caution that "not many of you should

---

[13]Ephesians 5:19.

[14]Colossians 3:16, NASB.

[15]Baurer, Arndt, Gingrich, Danker, *A Greek-English Lexicon of the New Testament and Other Early Christian Literature* (Chicago, IL: University of Chicago Press, 1979), 185.

[16]Allowing for questions and dialog is good. Not so good are endless bull sessions with off-the-cuff comments, unedifying add-ons, or allowing the undisciplined to go off topic.

[17]Teaching is listed as a spiritual gift in both Romans 12:7 and 1 Corinthians 12:28.

[18]Since 1 Timothy 2:12 prohibits women from teaching men, only brothers should be allowed to bring the lesson.

become teachers, my brothers, for you know that we who teach will be judged with greater strictness" makes sense in light of the participatory meetings that characterized the early church.[19]

Two or Three Tongues: The participatory nature of early church meetings is also evident in the guidelines concerning those who spoke in tongues: "If any speak in a tongue, let there be only two or at most three, and each in turn, and let someone interpret. But if there is no one to interpret, let each of them keep silent in church and speak to himself and to God."[20] An interpretation was required "so that the church might be built up."[21]

Speaking in tongues is a controversial topic.[22] Even if it is still for today, in many churches it would be inappropriate because it would not be edifying to the congregation. This is where the discernment of leaders is needed. However, the principle of participation remains. Brothers could still bring teachings, request or introduce songs, share testimonies, lead out in prayer, question the teacher, offer an encouraging word, etc.

Two or Three Prophets: No matter how you understand the gift of prophecy, the participatory nature of New Testament gatherings is seen in the guidelines for prophecy: "let two or three prophets speak, and let the others weigh what is said."[23] The impromptu nature of prophecy is clear: "If a revelation is made to another sitting there, let the first be silent."[24] The goal of prophecy is "so that all may learn and all be encouraged."[25]

"Prophet" is transliterated from *prophétés*; *pro* means before or forth and *phétés* means to speak. In general, prophets received divine revelation and passed it on. They proclaimed and interpreted divine truth.[26] This revelation may have concerned sin in someone's life (1Co 14:24-25), may have been

---

[19]James 3:1.
[20]1 Corinthians 14:27-28.
[21]1 Corinthians 14:5.
[22]If Charismatic churches followed the guidelines of 1 Corinthians 14 (a maximum of three, only one at a time, must be interpreted) much of what passes for legitimate tongues would be ruled out of order.
[23]1 Corinthians 14:29.
[24]1 Corinthians 14:30.
[25]1 Corinthians 14:31.
[26]Bauer, 723.

a word of encouragement (Acts 15:32) or may have been a prediction about the future (Acts 11:27-30).[27] Modern prophets might give practical insight into the correct application of Scripture. They are people of passion who speak forth words of encouragement, exhortation, motivation and application. They are agents for change who impart life into small church meetings.[28]

Prophecy and teaching were completely different gifts.[29] Though both resulted in learning and encouragement, prophets tended to get their messages by direct revelation from the Spirit whereas teachers spent hours in the study of written revelation (Scripture). As the source of a prophet's message was somewhat subjective, his revelations had to be judged (1Co 14:29b, 1Th 5:20-21).

PROFESSORS

In the *Mid-America Baptist Theological Journal*, Dr. Jimmy Milikin stated that in early Christian congregations "there was apparently a free expression of the Spirit. In the public assembly one person might have a psalm, another brother a teaching, another a revelation, another a tongue, another an interpretation."[30]

Church historian Ernest Scott wrote in *The Nature of the Early Church* that "The exercise of the spiritual gifts was thus the characteristic element in the primitive worship. Those gifts might vary in their nature and degree according to the capacity of each individual, but they were bestowed on all and room was allowed in the service for the participation of all who were present ... Every member was expected to contribute something of his own to the common worship."[31]

[27]To learn more about prophecy, see *The Gift of Prophecy in the New Testament and Today* by Wayne Grudem.

[28]It is the elders' duty to save the church from needless vexation by the emotionally unstable that fancy themselves prophets and would give weekly warnings of atomic holocaust.

[29]Romans 12: 6-7, 1 Corinthians 12:28.

[30]Jimmy Milikin, "Disorder Concerning Public Worship," *Mid America Baptist Theological Journal* (Memphis, TN: Mid-America Baptist Seminary Press, 1983), 125.

[31]Ernest Scott, *The Nature Of The Early Church* (New York, NY: Charles Scribner's Sons, 1941), 79.

Professor John Drane, in *Introducing the New Testament*, wrote, "In the earliest days ... their worship was spontaneous. This seems to have been regarded as the ideal, for when Paul describes how a church meeting should proceed he depicts a Spirit-led participation by many ... There was the fact that anyone had the freedom to participate in such worship. In the ideal situation, when everyone was inspired by the Holy Spirit, this was the perfect expression of Christian freedom."[32]

Concerning public worship in the New Testament church, London Bible College lecturer G.W. Kirby concluded, "There appears to have been considerable fluidity with time given for spontaneous participation."[33] William Barclay pointed out that "The really notable thing about an early Church service must have been that almost everyone came feeling that he had both the privilege and obligation of contributing something to it."[34]

PERSPECTIVE

It is helpful to have a good perspective on why participatory worship is important and how it was lost. After Christianity was made the official religion of the Roman Empire by Theodosius (around A.D. 381), huge pagan temples were turned by government decree into church buildings. Church gatherings moved out of the relative intimacy of Roman villas and into large, impersonal basilicas. Such huge gatherings naturally morphed into more of a performance or service. Socratic teaching gave way to eloquently orated monologs. Questions from the audience were prohibited. Spontaneity was lost. Individual participation was squelched. The "one another" aspect of an assembly became impractical. Informality fossilized into formality. Church leaders began wearing special clerical costumes. Worship aids were introduced: incense,

---

[32]John Drane, *Introducing the New Testament* (Oxford, UK: Lion Publishing, 1999), 402.

[33]G.W. Kirby, *Zondervan Pictorial Encyclopedia of the Bible*, Vol. 1 (Grand Rapids, IL: Zondervan 1982), p. 850.

[34]William Barclay, *The Letters to the Corinthians* (Philadelphia: Westminster Press, 1977), 135. Barclay's "everyone" needs qualification. The Scripture states that each one of the "brothers" was free to contribute something (1Co 14:26). For more in this see Appendix A.

icons, candles, hand gestures, etc. Church of Scotland minister Henry Sefton, in *A Lion Handbook - The History of Christianity*, wrote, "Worship in the house-church had been of an intimate kind in which all present had taken an active part ... (this) changed from being 'a corporate action of the whole church' into 'a service said by the clergy to which the laity listened.' "[35]

Many judge traditional worship services to be participatory simply because the congregation joins in responsive readings, partakes of the elements of the Lord's Supper, enjoys congregational singing, and gives financial offerings. These things are good, but there is no real open format. Commenting on the contrast between early and modern church meetings, Gordon Fee observed, "By and large the history of the church points to the fact that in worship we do not greatly trust the diversity of the body. Edification must always be the rule, and that carries with it orderliness so that all may learn and all be encouraged. But it is no great credit to the historical church that in opting for 'order' it also opted for a silencing of the ministry of the many."[36]

Not allowing the ministry of the many could cause atrophy and even apathy. A Sunday-school teacher once asked her children, "Why must we be quiet in church?" One perceptive little girl replied, "Because people are sleeping in there." Many feel they may as well stay home and watch a church service on television.

Allowing members to participate verbally in church lends for a greater working of the Spirit as the various ministry gifts are freed to function. Based on what Paul wrote in 1 Corinthians 14, God may burden a number of brothers, independently of each other, to bring a short word of encouragement, a testimony, to lead out in prayer, to bring a song, etc. Additional applications and illustrations can be offered by the body at large to augment a word of instruction. Allow brothers to ask questions or make comments during or after the teaching time. New believers learn how to think with

---

[35]Henry Sefton, *A Lion Handbook-The History of Christianity* (Oxford, UK: Lion Publishing, 1988), 151.
[36]Gordon Fee, NICNT, *The First Epistle To The Corinthians* (Grand Rapids: Wm. B. Eerdmans Publishing Co., 1987), 698.

the mind of Christ as they observe the more mature believers share in the meeting. Maturity skyrockets. The brothers begin to own the meeting, taking responsibility for the flow of the meeting as they become active participants rather than passive spectators. Edification is accomplished. (See Appendix B for practical examples).

PROPOSITION

The proposition is that you consider introducing participatory worship to your church. Perhaps you find the idea of participatory worship informative, but not worth the anticipated problems it might create. In response, it might be pointed out that where there are no oxen the barn is clean, but much increase comes from their strength.[37] The potential blessing is worth the risk. Beware the seven last words of declining churches: "We never did it that way before."

Some in Corinth wanted to conduct their meetings differently than 1 Corinthians 14 requires. In response, two questions were asked of them: "Or was it from you that the word of God came? Or are you the only ones it has reached?"[38] The word of God clearly did not originate with the Corinthians and they most certainly were not the only people it had reached. (As such, whatever applied to the Corinthian church would apply to us as well.) These questions were designed to convince the Corinthian believers they had no authority to conduct their meetings in any other way than that prescribed by the apostles. The Scripture does not prohibit participatory worship; it regulates it.

There are to be edifying contributions and encouraging input by those who gather. When giving guidelines for participatory worship, Paul wrote, "the things I am writing to you are a command of the Lord" (1Co 14:37). A command is not a suggestion. It is more than a good idea. The instructions in 1 Corinthians are not merely interesting history. These participatory regulations are not merely descriptive of primitive church meetings; in some sense, they are prescriptive. How

---

[37]Proverbs 14:4.
[38]1 Corinthians 14:36.

will you lead your church to obey the command of the Lord regarding participatory worship?

Is the time the body comes together supposed to be focused only on one or two leaders or is it an opportunity for God to speak through multiple brothers to those gathered? Often when a gifted pastor leaves a church, attendance plummets. Distributing the focus to multiple men speaking strengthens the church as a whole. The church is not so dependent on the gifting of just one man. The chances of a personality cult developing are lessened. One of Martin Luther's points of reformation concerned the priesthood of all believers. Do we really believe in the priesthood of the believer? If so, perhaps we could prove it by allowing the priests to carry out their ministries in the church meetings.

One home field advantage small churches have is the very real possibility of experiencing truly edifying participatory worship. When managed properly by the elders, open worship taps into the spiritual gifts of the congregation. People get excited about coming, as they can meaningfully contribute to the meeting or be blessed by what others share. Sometimes, God will speak a complete message through His people during a meeting where the testimonies, teaching, songs, and encouragement all mesh beautifully together—many springs combining into one river. Promoting "one anothering" in the assembly can be a great encouragement to those involved with small churches. Why would Scripture speak of these things if they were not important? Participatory worship can take small church meetings from ordinary to extraordinary.

See Appendix B for practical ideas on implementing participatory worship.

Go to NTRF.org for more information on participatory worship (audio, articles, teacher discussion guide, etc.).

DISCUSSION QUESTIONS

1. Taken as a whole, what are the various indicators throughout 1 Corinthians 14 that combine to show the participatory nature of early church meetings?

2. Suppose 1 Corinthians 14:26 was a criticism of what the Corinthian church was doing; why is it significant that the inspired solution was a regulation of participatory meetings rather than a prohibition of them?

3. Why is it important for everything said and done in the church meeting to be edifying? *See 1 Corinthians 14:1-25.*

4. What are some of the guiding principles for participatory church meetings, based on 1 Corinthians 14 and Hebrews 10:24-25?

5. What role should elders play in participatory meetings? *See 1 Timothy 1:3-5, 3:5, 4:11-14, 5:17, 6:2b, 2 Timothy 4:1-2, Titus 2:1, 2:15.*

6. What can be done if week after week few brothers share anything of significance in participatory worship?

7. Why would the absence of charismatic gifts not nullify the general principle of participatory church meetings?

8. What is it that the Lord is commanding in 1 Corinthians 14:37?

9. What are some appropriate contributions to a church meeting, based on Acts 2:42, Acts 14:26-28 and 1 Timothy 4:13?

10. Why would a smaller congregation have an advantage over a huge one when it comes to participatory worship?

3

ELDER RULE & CONGREGATIONAL CONSENSUS – DANCE PARTNERS

What is the advantage of following the early church's approach to decision making? *No matter who has the final authority to make decisions in your church, adopting early church attitudes can make the process both unifying and edifying.* An important role of first-century church leaders was to build congregational consensus.

PROFIT

The mind of Christ is more likely found when the leaders guide the whole congregation to wrestle corporately with major decisions. Unity is strengthened. The Spirit is given free rein to guide the church. Leadership's role in this process includes helping to build consensus by teaching what Scripture says on various issues, privately talking with church members about decisions, appealing to those who differ and—after much persuasion—calling on any dissenting minority to yield to the elders along with the rest of the congregation. Church members are encouraged and fulfilled as they realize that everyone's thoughts and inputs are respectfully weighed in accordance with Scripture.

PROOF #1—A LEADER'S AUTHORITY

Perhaps the best place to begin a study of authority within the church is with the words of our Lord. Contrasting the authority of political leaders with church leaders, Jesus said:

"The kings of the Gentiles exercise lordship over them, and those in authority over them are called benefactors. But not so with you. Rather, let the greatest among you become as the youngest, and the leader as one who serves."[1] Think about that a minute. How much authority does the youngest person in a family have? How much authority does a household servant have? Jesus gave examples of those in Roman society who had the least authority—children and slaves. Although it is true that Jesus was a master of overstatement, there is an underlying truth that must not be glossed over. Church leaders are to be servant leaders. Their attitude should be one of humility in leadership, not kingly authority that lords over people. In harmony with Jesus' words, Peter later instructed elders to "shepherd the flock of God ... not domineering over those in your charge, but being examples to the flock."[2]

An elder must lead with a servant's heart. Jesus offered Himself as an example for church leaders to follow: "Who is the greater, one who reclines at table or one who serves? Is it not the one who reclines at table? But I am among you as the one who serves."[3] On another occasion, Jesus washed the disciples' feet. Why did He do this? It was to make the point that anyone who wants to be a church leader must first learn to be the servant of all. He said: "You call me Teacher and Lord, and you are right, for so I am. If I then, your Lord and Teacher, have washed your feet, you also ought to wash one another's feet. For I have given you an example, that you also should do just as I have done to you. Truly, truly, I say to you, a servant is not greater than his master, nor is a messenger greater than the one who sent him. If you know these things, blessed are you if you do them."[4] Do you want God's blessing on you as a church leader? Then do what Jesus modeled and wield your authority with a servant's heart.

PROOF #2—SHEPHERDS ARE SHEEP TOO

Church leaders were given little prominence in the epistles. Paul's highly theological epistle to the Romans was

---

[1] Luke 22:25-26.
[2] 1 Peter 5:1-3.
[3] Luke 22:27.
[4] John 13:13-17.

addressed simply to the "saints" in Rome (1:7), with no special mention of the shepherds. In Romans 13, Paul brought up submission to the civil government, but never mentioned the church submitting to its elders. In Romans 15, Paul expressed to the whole church his intent to visit. Can you imagine the indignation that would take place today if someone like Billy Graham wrote to an entire church that he was soon to visit, rather than writing specifically to its leaders?

The two letters to the Corinthian congregation were addressed to the entire "church" (1Co 1:2, 2Co 1:1), with no mention of its leaders in the greetings or anywhere throughout the entirety of the letters. This is all the more remarkable when one considers that these two epistles deal with many leadership matters: church discipline, marriage, divorce and remarriage, abuse of the Lord's Supper, giving, and how to conduct a worship service.

The greeting in Galatians 1:2 was to all the "churches" in the region of Galatia, with no mention of any leadership. The readers were addressed throughout the book simply as "brothers." This is because shepherds are sheep, too.

The "saints in Ephesus" were the designated recipients of that letter (Ep 1:1). The importance of pastor-teachers was mentioned in 4:11, but pastor-teachers were not written to directly. If ever there was an appropriate place to instruct the church to submit to and obey its elders, it would arguably have been in Ephesians 5-6, where Paul instructed women to submit to their husbands, children to obey their parents, and slaves their masters. Yet it is missing. Could this be in keeping with Jesus' words that a church leader has the same authority as a child and slave?

Philippians 1:1 breaks the pattern of leadership neglect: the deacons and overseers were greeted along with the saints. However, no other mention was made of these leaders, nor was anything written directly to them in the letter.

The salutation of Colossians 1:2 was simply to "the saints and faithful brothers." Nothing was written directly to or even about the leaders. Chapters 3-4 parallel Ephesians 5-6 in dealing with the relationship between man and wife, parents and children, and slaves and masters. It would have been a logical place to write about the submission of a congregation to its leaders, yet nothing was written. Similarly, in 1 Peter 2-3, Peter dealt with a believer's submission to the government and a wife's submission to her husband, but, like Paul, wrote nothing about the church's submission to its leaders. In all the letters to the churches, it is not until 1 Peter 5 that elders are written to directly.[5]

This ignoring of the leadership is also seen in the salutations of the letters to the Thessalonians, James' letter to the twelve scattered tribes, Peter's and John's epistles, and Jude. All of this implies that the elders were themselves also sheep. The elders were a subset of the church as a whole. There was no clergy/laity distinction. In the very last chapter of Hebrews, the readers were asked to "greet all your leaders" (13:24). Not only did the author not greet the leaders directly, he assumed they would not even be reading the letter!

Much may be gleaned from the way that New Testament writers appealed directly to entire congregations. They went to great lengths to influence all believers, not just those in leadership. The apostles did not simply bark orders and issue injunctions (as a military commander might do). Instead, they treated other believers as equals and appealed directly to them as such. No doubt local church leaders led in much the same way. An elder's primary authority was in his ability to influence with the truth. The respect they were given was honestly earned. It was the opposite of military authority wherein soldiers respect the rank but not necessarily the man.

Hebrews 13:7 reflects the fact that the leadership style employed by church leaders is primarily one of direction by example: "Remember your leaders ... Consider the outcome of their way of life and imitate their faith." Along this same line, 1 Thessalonians 5:12-13 reveals that leaders are to be respected, not because of the automatic authority of appointed

[5]Timothy and Titus were not local pastors. They were apostolic workers, sent by Paul to various places to organize the churches and then to move on to other locations. The letters to Timothy and Titus are called "pastoral epistles" because of their emphasis on elders, their qualifications, and their duties.

rank, but because of the value of their service—"Hold them in highest regard in love because of their work." As Jesus said, "You know that the rulers of the Gentiles lord it over them, and their high officials exercise authority over them. Not so with you. Instead, whoever wants to become great among you must be your servant, and whoever wants to be first must be your slave" (Mt 20:25-28).

PROOF #3—BE PERSUADED & YIELD

Hebrews 13:17 instructs believers to *obey* church leaders.[6] However, mindless obedience is not what is pictured. The common Greek word for "obey" (*hupakouo*) was used with reference to such situations as children obeying their parents and slaves their masters.[7] However, the common word for "obey" is not found in Hebrews 13:17. Instead, the word used is *peitho*, which fundamentally means persuade or convince.[8] In Greek mythology, Peitho was the goddess who personified persuasion.[9] Consistent with this root meaning, McReynolds' literal interlinear translates *peitho* as "persuade" in Hebrews 13:17.[10] The expositor Vine went a step further and stated that with *peitho*, "the obedience suggested is not by submission to authority, but resulting from persuasion."[11] Lenski's comment on this text is that if one allows oneself to be convinced by someone, one obeys him.[12] In our passage, it is found in the present imperative passive form, which takes on the meaning "obey."[13] However, the author's use of *peitho* may suggest that dialog will take place, teaching will be given, and arguments

---

[6]The New Testament usually refers to church leaders in the plural. The idea of a single pastor over a congregation was foreign to the early church.

[7]Ephesians 6:1, 5.

[8]Baurer, Arndt, Gingrich, Danker, *A Greek-English Lexicon of the New Testament and Other Early Christian Literature* (Chicago, IL: University of Chicago Press, 1979), 639. Other examples of *peitho* are found in Luke 16:31, Acts 17:4 and 21:14.

[9]"Peitho", en.Wikipedia.org. Accessed October 5, 2017.

[10]Paul McReynolds, *Word Study Greek-English New Testament* (Wheaton, IL: Tyndale Publishers, 1999), 819.

[11]W.E. Vine, *An Expository Dictionary of New Testament Words* (Iowa Falls, IA: Riverside Book and Bible House, 1952), 124.

[12]R.C.H. Lenski, *The Interpretation of the Epistle to the Hebrews and the Epistle of James* (Minneapolis, MN: Augsburg Publishing, 1966), 490.

[13]Horst Balz & Gerhard Schneider, eds., *Exegetical Dictionary of the New Testament*, Vol. 3, (Grand Rapids, MI: William B. Eerdmans Publishing, 1993), 63.

will be made in order to bring about this obedience. When someone is persuaded of something, he will act on it and, in that sense, obey it with joyful conviction.

One of the qualifications of an elder is that he should be able to teach.[14] This is because church leaders have to be eminently good at persuading with the truth. Dwight Eisenhower captured the idea behind Hebrews 13:17 when he said, "I would rather try to persuade a man to go along, because once I have persuaded him he will stick. If I scare him, he will stay just as long as he is scared, and then he is gone."[15] Elders are not to simply pronounce decisions from on high like Popes, ex cathedra. Ideally, the obedience of Hebrews 13:17 happens after a process of persuasion.

Hebrews 13:17 further instructs believers to *submit* to their church leaders. However, the common Greek word for "submit" (*hupotasso*) is not found here.[16] Instead, the classical Greek word *hupeiko* was chosen by the author, a synonym for *hupotasso* that means to give way or to yield.[17] Rienecker defined it as "to give in, to yield, to submit."[18] *Hupeiko* was used elsewhere of combatants and meant to yield after a struggle. The nuance of *hupeiko* is not a structure to which one automatically submits (like submission to civil government). Rather, it is submission after a process, struggle, or contest has occurred. The picture is one of serious discussion and dialog prior to one party giving way.[19]

In summary, mindless slave-like obedience is not the relationship presented in the New Testament between leaders and those led. For their part, God's flock must be open to being persuaded (*peitho*) by its shepherds. Leaders, in turn, must be committed to ongoing discussion and teaching. However, there will be those times when someone, or some few, in the fellowship can't be persuaded. Congregations are

---

[14]1 Timothy 3:2.

[15]QuotationsPage.com, #2662, accessed September 30, 2016.

[16]Used for instance in Romans 13:1, Colossians 3:18, Ephesians 5:21, and 1 Peter 2:13.

[17]Baurer, 838.

[18]Fritz Rienecker & Cleon Rogers, *Linguistic Key to the Greek New Testament* (Grand Rapids, MI: Zondervan Publishing, 1980), 720.

[19]Hal Miller, "As Children and Slaves: Authority in the NT", NextReformation. com. Accessed October 05, 2017.

made up of both mature and immature Christians, of those who walk in the Spirit and those who do not, of those with the gift of discernment and those without it—so impasses will arise. After much persuasion and prayer, Hebrews 13:17 calls on dissenters to give in to, to yield to (*hupeiko*), the wisdom of church leaders. This submission, however, is to come only after dialogue, discussion, and reasoning. Thus, a critical aspect of elder rule must include a commitment to building Spirit-filled congregational consensus.

PROOF #4—CHURCH AS CONGRESS

Our understanding of Christ's church will be impoverished if we fail to factor in the dynamics of the original Greek word for church, *ekklésia*. With so much emphasis today on the separation of church and state, the last thing people associate church with is government. Yet *ekklésia* was a government word in its original, secular setting. In Jesus' day, *ekklésia* was used outside the New Testament to refer to a political assembly that was regularly convened for the purpose of making decisions.[20] According to Thayer, it was "an assembly of the people convened at the public place of council for the purpose of deliberation."[21] Bauer's lexicon defines *ekklésia* as an "assembly of a regularly summoned political body."[22] Lothan Coenen, writing for *The New International Dictionary of New Testament Theology*, noted that *ekklésia* was "clearly characterized as a political phenomenon, repeated according to certain rules and within a certain framework. It was the assembly of full citizens, functionally rooted in the constitution of the democracy, an assembly in which fundamental political and judicial decisions were taken ... the word *ekklésia*, throughout the Greek and Hellenistic areas, always retained its reference to the assembly of the polis."[23]

---

[20]Within the Scriptures, *ekklésia* was also used to simply refer a gathering (of Israel or the church), to the church as the totality of Christians living in one place and to the universal church to which all believers belong.
[21]Thayer, 196.
[22]Baurer, 240.
[23]Lothan Coenen, "Church", *The New International Dictionary of New Testament Theology*, Vol. 1, Colin Brown, General Editor (Grand Rapids, MI: Zondervan, 1971), 291.

The secular meaning of *ekklésia* can be seen in Acts 19, where it is translated as "legal assembly" rather than as "church."[24] Two of the occurrences in Acts 19 refer to a meeting of silversmiths convened by Demetrius. Trade union members rushed into the theater (where civic decisions were normally made) to decide what to do about a damaged reputation and lost business.[25] However, they overstepped their jurisdiction, so the town clerk counseled that the matter be settled by the "legal" *ekklesia*, rather than by the trade union *ekklesia* (Acts 19:37-39).

Why did Jesus choose such a politically loaded word (*ekklésia*) to describe His people and their meetings?[26] Had He merely wanted to describe a gathering with no political connotations, Jesus could have used *sunagogé*, *thiasos* or *eranos*. Perhaps Jesus intended His followers to function together with a purpose somehow parallel to that of the political government. If so, believers have the responsibility to decide things together and experience the consensus process. God's people have a decision-making mandate. A church is a body of Kingdom citizens authorized to weigh major issues, make decisions, and pass judgments on various issues. Thus, according to the *Baptist Faith and Message* of 2000, "Each congregation operates under the Lordship of Christ through democratic processes."[27]

There are many examples in the New Testament of God's people making decisions as a body. After promising to build His *ekklésia* on the rock of Peter's revealed confession, Jesus immediately spoke of the keys of the kingdom of heaven and of binding and loosing (Mt 16:13-20). Keys represent the ability to open and to close something, "kingdom" is a political term, and binding and loosing involves the authority to make decisions. Was this authority given to Peter only? In Matthew 18:15-20, binding and loosing authority was conferred by Jesus on the whole *ekklésia*. In Acts 1:15-26, Peter charged the Jerusalem church as a whole with finding a replacement for

---

[24]Acts 19:32, 39, 41 (NIV).
[25]"Theater," Ephesus.us, accessed September 1, 2016. There was so much confusion the majority did not know why they had been summoned.
[26]Matthew 16:13-20 & 18:15-20. In the Septuagint, wilderness gatherings of the ancient Israelites were called an *ekklesia*.
[27]Article VI, "The Church."

Judas. Later, the apostles looked to the church corporately to pick men to administer the church's food program (Acts 6:1-6). Acts 14:23 indicated the apostles appointed elders with the consensus of the local congregation.[28]

If ever there were a proper time and place for the Apostles to make a decision alone, apart from the church, it was at the Jerusalem Council (Acts 15). The Apostles were the standard for doctrine and practice. The very nature of the Gospel had been called into question. Yet, even here, the amazing fact is that the Apostles not only included the local Jerusalem elders but also the whole church![29] Colin Brown observed that "in the council's decision-making they are accorded no special preeminence ... It is consistent with the non-authoritarian, collegiate character of church leadership which Acts consistently depicts (1:13-26; 6:2ff; 8:14ff; 11:1ff; 13:1-4)."[30] Furthermore, 1 Corinthians 5 also reveals the church corporately has the authority to lovingly discipline unrepentant members for their possible future restoration and for the holiness of the church.

PROFESSORS

Church government is one area of early church practice where there is little scholarly agreement. G.W. Kirby, lecturer in practical theology at London Bible College, wrote that "The NT does not lay down precise rules either as to the form of ministry or of government of the Church. Over the centuries several different theories of church government have emerged, each of which claims some scriptural basis."[31] However, commenting on the general nature of congregational involvement, Donald Guthrie observed, "These early communities displayed a remarkable virility, which was a particular characteristic of that age. The churches were living organisms rather than organizations. The promptings of the Spirit were more important than ecclesiastical edicts or

---

[28]"Paul and Barnabas had elders elected" (footnoted alternative translation, NIV).
[29]Acts 15:4, 12, 22.
[30]Colin Brown, Vol. 1, *Dictionary of New Testament Theology* (Grand Rapids, MI: Zondervan, 1981), 135.
[31]G.W. Kirby, *The Zondervan Pictorial Encyclopedia of the Bible* (Grand Rapids, MI: Zondervan, 1982), 854.

Episcopal pronouncements. When decisions were made, they were made by the whole company of believers, not simply by the officials ... It would be a mistake, nevertheless, to suppose because of this that the church was run on democratic lines. The Acts record makes unmistakably clear that the dominating factor was the guidance of the Holy Spirit."[32]

Regardless of your church's process of government, the New Testament approach would be for leaders to involve the whole church in big decisions, depending on the Holy Spirit and seeking to build congregational consensus in matters of importance. Examples include church discipline, deciding on a new meeting place, changing a doctrinal stance, appointing new elders and deacons, deciding which missions to support, or altering how church meetings are held. Early church government was a combination of plural elder rule and congregational consensus as Christ was followed as Head.

PROVISION

It is important to remember that the process a church goes through in achieving consensus may be just as important as the consensus that is finally achieved. Consensus governing takes time, commitment, mutual edification, and lots of brotherly love. It truly *can* work in smaller churches, such as were found in the New Testament era. [33] We must love each other enough to put up with each other and work through disagreements. The concept of consensus might be called government by unity, oneness, harmony, or mutual agreement. Do we really trust in the Holy Spirit to work in our lives and churches?

Lest achieving consensus seem too utopian, consider what the Lord has done to help His people. First, our Lord Himself prayed "that they may be one as we are one ... that all of them may be one, Father, just as you are in me and

---

[32]Donald Guthrie, *New Testament Theology* (Downers Grove, IL: Inter-Varsity Press, 1981), 741.

[33]Because the early church met in the private homes of its wealthier members, each congregation was necessarily smaller rather than larger (scores of people rather than hundreds or thousands).

I am in you ... May they be brought into complete unity" (Jn 17:11, 20-23). Because Jesus prayed this for us, unity is certainly achievable.

Another provision God made for our unity lies in the Lord's Supper. According to 1 Corinthians 10:17, "Because there is one loaf, we, who are many, are one body, for we all partake of the one loaf." Examine the prepositions in 1 Corinthians 10:17 ("because" and "for"); partaking of the Lord's Supper not only pictures unity, it may even create it.[34]

Finally, Christ gave the church various leadership gifts (such as pastor-teacher) for a purpose: "until we all reach unity in the faith" (Ep 4:11-13). Leaders play a critical role in building consensus. Aristotle astutely realized that "we believe good men more fully and more readily than others. This is true generally whatever the question is, and absolutely true where exact certainty is impossible and opinions are divided ... his character may almost be called the most effective means of persuasion he possesses."[35]

PROPOSITION

The church as a whole may be compared to a congress with authority to make decisions and render judgments that are binding on its members. Church leaders are congressman also but appointed to a special committee whose purpose is to study issues, make recommendations, teach, inform, or prompt the congress. Church leaders should not normally make fiat decisions on behalf of the church in lieu of the consensus process. Elders should guide, teach, suggest, and build consensus. However, when the church finds itself in gridlock, unable to resolve an issue, the elders serve as predetermined arbitrators, or tiebreakers. In these instances, those in opposition are called on to submit in the Lord to the elders' leadership and wisdom (Heb 13:17). Spirit-filled elder rule combined with congregational consensus in major decisions gives free reign to the Holy Spirit and puts the church in a better

---

[34]More can be read on this in Appendix C and at NTRF.org.

[35]*Aristotle's Rhetoric*, Book 1, Chapter 2.

position to discern the mind of Christ and to walk in the Light of God's Word.

Appendix C contains practical thoughts on elder-led congregational consensus.

Articles, audio, and a teacher's discussion guide on elder rule and congregational consensus can be found at NTRF.org.

DISCUSSION QUESTIONS

1. What can be learned about a church leader's authority from Luke 22:24-27?

2. To what did the Greek word *ekklésia* originally refer?

3. Why do you suppose that Jesus chose a political word like *ekklésia* to describe His followers?

4. What are some examples in the New Testament of God's people making decisions as a body?

5. What is the difference between majority rule and congregational consensus?

6. What is the difference between consensus and unanimity?

7. What provisions has God made to help a church achieve consensus?

8. How do elders build congregational consensus?

9. In Hebrews 13:17 believers are encouraged to obey and submit to their leaders. How does this square with congregational rule?

10. How should both local church congregational consensus and universal church consensus apply to interpreting the Bible?

4

SMALL CHURCHES
– A DIVINE DESIGN

First-century Christians gathered almost exclusively in private homes. God used these house churches to turn the Roman world upside down.[1] Could He use small congregations today as strategically as He did early house churches? *Small churches that do the types of things first-century house churches did, in the love and power of the Holy Spirit, have great potential to advance God's kingdom.* Small and Spirit-filled is part of a divine design.

PROFIT

Since everything in the New Testament was written to churches that met in the private homes of its members, the relationship dynamics it describes work best in smaller settings. Smaller settings foster the intimacy, unity, love and accountability that characterized the early church. The relationships described in the New Testament work best in situations where everyone knows each other. A loving, family-like atmosphere is more easily developed. The many "one another" exhortations of Scripture can be more realistically lived out. Church discipline takes on genuine significance. Disciple making is personal and natural. Participatory worship fits smaller settings better and the things shared are much more meaningful. Celebrating the Lord's Supper as an actual family meal is more natural in a smaller setting. Achieving congregational consensus is easier when everyone knows everyone else and open lines of communication genuinely exist with one another. Involvement with a smaller church can be a wonderful blessing with strategic, divinely designed advantages.

---

[1]Acts 17:6.

PROOF

Scripture indicates the early church met in the private homes of its more affluent members. Philemon, wealthy enough to own a slave, hosted a church in his home (Phlm 2b). Church hostess Lydia was a prosperous businesswoman who sold expensive purple fabric and could afford servants (Ac 16:14). A church met in the home of Aquila and Priscilla, a couple employed in the evidently lucrative first-century trade of tent-making (Ac 18:1-3).[2] Gaius, a man with the means to generously support missionaries (3Jn 1-5), had a home big enough to host the sizable Corinthian congregation (Ro 16:23). According to Yale University archaeologists, "The first Christian congregations worshipped in private houses, meeting at the homes of wealthier members on a rotating basis ... Worship was generally conducted in the atrium, or central courtyard of the house."[3]

Less well known is the fact the early church continued this practice of home meetings for hundreds of years after the New Testament was completed. Graydon Snyder of Chicago Theological Seminary observed that "the New Testament Church began as a small group house church (Col. 4:15), and it remained so until the middle or end of the third century. There are no evidences of larger places of meeting before 300."[4] Again quoting Snyder, "there is no literary evidence nor archaeological indication that any such home was converted into an extant church building. Nor is there any extant church that certainly was built prior to Constantine."[5]

The real issue is not where a church meets but how it can best do what God requires of it. Size plays an important role in this. Having too many people in attendance can serve to defeat the purposes for holding a church meeting in the first place. Large crowds are great for special praise concerts, seminars, or evangelism but the weekly church gathering is to

[2]Through his tent making work, Paul was able to support himself and his traveling companions, some seven men at least (Acts 20:4, 34).
[3]"Unearthing the Christian Building", *Dura-Europos: Excavating Antiquity* (Yale University Art Gallery), 2.
[4]Graydon F. Synder, *Church Life Before Constantine* (Macon, GA: Mercer University Press, 1991), 166.
[5]Ibid., 67.

be about something more: mutual edification, accountability, encouraging one another, the fellowship of the Holy Meal, strengthening relationships, building consensus, etc. In keeping with the New Testament example, the ideal size for a congregation might be the same number of people that would fit into a first-century Roman villa.

PROFESSORS

Reformed scholar William Hendriksen said, "since in the first and second centuries church buildings in the sense in which we think of them today were not yet in existence, families would hold services in their own homes."[6] (By services, Hendriksen did not mean personal family devotions, but church services in a private home).

According to Anglican priest and evangelist David Watson, "For the first two centuries, the church met in small groups in the homes of its members, apart from special gatherings in public lecture halls or market places, where people could come together in much larger numbers. Significantly these two centuries mark the most powerful and vigorous advance of the church, which perhaps has never seen been equaled."[7]

Martin Selman of Spurgeon's College in London wrote, "The theme of the 'household of God' undoubtedly owed much to the function of the house in early Christianity as a place of meeting and fellowship (e.g. 2 Tim. 4:19; Phm. 2; 2 Jn. 10)."[8]

According to W.H. Griffith Thomas, co-founder of Dallas Theological Seminary, "For two or three centuries Christians met in private houses ... There seems little doubt that these informal gatherings of small groups of believers had great influence in preserving the simplicity and purity of early Christianity."[9]

---

[6] William Hendriksen, *New Testament Commentary on Romans* (Grand Rapids, MI: Baker Book House), 22.

[7] David Watson, *I Believe in the Church* (Great Britain: Hodder & Stoughton, 1978), 121.

[8] J. D. Douglas, ed. *New Bible Dictionary* (Wheaton, IL: Tyndale, 1982), 498.

[9] W.H. Griffith Thomas, *St. Paul's Epistle to the Romans* (Grand Rapids, MI: Eerdmans Publishing, 1984), 422-423.

Seminary professor Ronald Sider, in *Rich Christians in an Age of Hunger*, wrote, "The early church was able to defy the decadent values of Roman civilization precisely because it experienced the reality of Christian fellowship in a mighty way ... Christian fellowship meant unconditional availability to and unlimited liability for the other sisters and brothers—emotionally, financially and spiritually. When one member suffered, they all suffered. When one rejoiced, they all rejoiced (1 Cor. 12:26). When a person or church experienced economic trouble, the others shared without reservation. And when a brother or sister fell into sin, the others gently restored the straying person (Mt. 18:15-17; 1 Cor. 5; 2 Cor. 2:5-11; Gal. 6:1-3). The sisters and brothers were available to each other, liable for each other and accountable to each other. The early church, of course, did not always fully live out the New Testament vision of the body of Christ. There were tragic lapses. But the network of tiny house churches scattered throughout the Roman Empire did experience their oneness in Christ so vividly that they were able to defy and eventually conquer a powerful, pagan civilization. The overwhelming majority of churches today, however, do not provide the context in which brothers and sisters can encourage, admonish and disciple each other. We desperately need new settings and structures for watching over one another in love."[10]

PATTERN

What are we to do with the fact that the early church met mostly in homes? The most common explanation for the existence of early house churches was the pressure of persecution, similar to the situation existing today in China or Iran. Yet even in the absence of persecution, might the apostles have intended to lay down a purposeful pattern of smaller congregations? It is a design axiom that form follows function. Meeting in a smaller setting would have a practical effect on one's church life. The apostles' belief concerning the function of the church was

---

[10]Ronald Sider, *Rich Christians in an Age of Hunger* (Downers Grove, IL: IVP, 1977), 190-191.

naturally expressed in the form the church took on in the first century. Some of the distinct practices of those early small churches are worth considering: [11]

1. **The Church as Family:** An overarching significance of the New Testament church lies in its theology of community. The church was depicted by apostolic writers in terms which describe a family. Believers are children of God (1Jn 3:1) who have been born into his family (Jn 1:12-13). God's people are thus seen as part of God's household (Ep 2:19, Ga 6:10). They are called brothers and sisters (Phm 2, Ro 16:2). Consequently, Christians are to relate to each other as members of a family (1Ti 5:1-2; Ro 16:13). Out of the theological truth that God's children are family arises many church practice issues, such as the size of a congregation that best facilities our functioning as God's family. According to Fuller seminary professor Robert Banks, "Even the meetings of the 'whole church' were small enough for a relatively intimate relationship to develop between the members."[12]

2. **One Another Ministry:** The Scriptures are full of "one another" commands.[13] The Church should be associated with mutual encouragement, accountability, relationships, community and maintaining church discipline. These ideals are best accomplished in smaller congregations where people know and love each other. A large auditorium of people, most of whom are relative strangers to each other, will not easily achieve these goals. Nominal Christianity is harbored as it becomes easy to get lost in the crowd. Smaller churches can best foster the simplicity, vitality, intimacy and purity that God desires for His Church.

3. **Participatory Worship:** Early church meetings were clearly participatory. As public speaking is a great fear,

---

[11]Special thanks to Stephen David of Hyderabad, India for significant contributions to this section.

[12]Robert Banks, *Paul's Idea of Community: The Early House Churches in Their Historical Setting* (Grand Rapids, MI: Eerdmans Publishing, 1988), 41-42.

[13]There are over fifty of them, such as love one another, give preference to one another, encourage one another, agree with one another, accept one another, submit to one another, etc.

participatory meetings are best suited to smaller gatherings composed of people who all know each other and are true friends. After church meetings in Roman atriums were replaced by meetings in much larger basilicas, participatory worship was replaced by scripted, stage performance type services. The practical reality of the priesthood of the believer was lost until the Reformation.

4. **The Holy Meal:** The Lord's Supper was originally celebrated weekly as a full, fellowship meal (the *Agapé* Feast). Each local church is to be like a family; one of the most common things families do is eat together. The larger the congregation, the less family-like and the more impersonal the Lord's Supper as a true meal becomes. Early church meetings centered on the Lord's Table were tremendous times of fellowship, community, and encouragement. Rather than in a funeral-like atmosphere, the Lord's Supper was reverently celebrated in anticipation of the Wedding Banquet of the Lamb.

5. **Congregational Consensus:** The New Testament church had a plurality of clearly identified leaders (elders, pastors, overseers), yet these leaders led more by example and persuasion than by command. Building consensus of the whole congregation was important in decision making. Achieving consensus is possible in a church where everyone knows each other, loves each other, bears with one another, is patient with one another and is committed to each other. An informal, smaller setting is an effective place for the building of consensus. However, the larger the fellowship, the more difficult it becomes to maintain relationships and lines of communication. Further, in a large congregation, the pastor necessarily functions more like the CEO of a corporation or, worse yet, like a king over his own kingdom. The pastors become inaccessible. Intimacy is lost.

6. **Multiplication:** Small churches have great potential for growth through multiplication. New churches grow faster than larger ones.[14] New leaders should be continually trained

---

[14]"Why Do Newly Planted Churches Grow Faster Than Older Churches?", rmdc. org, accessed September 1, 2016.

from within to go out and start new works. We need to think small in a really big way! Rather than growing a single church bigger and bigger, consider sending off clusters of people to start new small churches. Commit to being a small church that starts new small churches that start other small churches.

7. **Resource Allocation:** Charles Price, Director of Missions for the San Antonio Baptist Association, lamented that the typical cost to start a new church in North America is an astounding two million dollars.[15] Jim Henry, pastor of First Baptist Church of Orlando estimated, "Our two church plants are going to cost us about $2,450,000 over a three-year period."[16] In light of these staggering figures, as your small church starts new small churches, be creative in finding places to meet that are cost efficient. Look into renting an apartment clubhouse, dance academy, storefront, school cafeteria or community center. Kingdom minded older congregations may be willing to let you use their building after their services are over. Don't rule out the possibility of meeting in someone's home—under the right circumstances it can still be a viable option.[17]

PROPORTIONS

Just how many people were involved in an early house church? As New Testament churches met almost exclusively in private homes, the typical congregation of the apostolic era was relatively small.[18] There were no more people than would fit into a wealthy person's home (in the atrium, courtyard, or large living area). Though house churches were at the opposite end of the spectrum from modern mega-churches, it is important to avoid the mistake of thinking *too* small. The size should be just right; not too big and not too small (neither mega nor micro).

---

[15]E-mail exchange, May 8, 2013.
[16]"How Much Does It Cost To Start A Church?", MissionalChallenge.com, accessed September 1, 2016.
[17]The home should have a large assembly room and ample off-street parking.
[18]While it cannot be said for certain that every church met in a home, it is a fact that when a meeting place is specified in Scripture, it is in a home. Perhaps some congregations were large and therefore met in big buildings, but this is an argument from silence.

The Matthew 18 restoration process detailed by Jesus clearly assumes more than just "us four and no more." There was a single house church meeting in Corinth; counting the various people using their spiritual gifts in 1 Corinthians 14 adds up to a healthy number of believers. Early house churches were able to support qualified widows and elders, which would have required more than just a handful of believers (1Ti 5:3-16). Having a plurality of elders in a church is unlikely in too small a setting (Acts 14:23). Early churches meeting in Roman villas typically consisted of scores of people, perhaps over a hundred, but not hundreds and certainly not thousands.[19]

As already seen, Scripture indicates the early church met in the homes of its wealthier members.[20] This was probably because of the large size of the home and the ability of the host to provide much of the food for the love feast. The challenge in worshiping in a home today lies in the fact that modern homes are often far different from first-century Roman villas.

Roman villas doubled as centers for commerce. They were big, semipublic houses. The two rooms facing the street were often businesses. A hallway between them led into the home's atrium. At the far end of the atrium was the business office. It was not unusual for strangers to be in and out of a home. Further, there were typically multiple generations of family under the same roof. In addition, the household employed servants and their families.

There were large areas in which the church could gather, such as the atrium. Walls between adjoining rooms off the atrium could be removed to create a big open area. Beyond the business office was an even larger semi-covered and completely enclosed courtyard. Spacious living rooms were often built off the courtyard. Enough believers were able to gather in the villas to make disciples, manifest a variety of spiritual gifts, have multiple people with the same gift, give to widows and orphans, have a plurality of elders and financially support

---

[19]The Jerusalem Church had thousands of members meeting house to house.
[20]Acts 16:40, 20:20, Romans 16:3-5a, 16:23, 1 Corinthians 16:19, Colossians 4:15, Philemon 1-2b, James 2:3. Though Scripture never states such, it is quite likely that churches also met in tenement housing called *insula* and which were not nearly as large as a Roman villa.

qualified pastor-teachers (who were, thus, freed to be devoted to making disciples, in-depth teaching and leadership). They also probably had more of an Asian mindset to crowding than we do in the West; there may have been 150 people in an early house church.

The meeting room of the Lullingstone Villa house church in Kent, England (built during the Roman occupation) measured approximately 15' x 21'.[21] By modern standards this would seat about 50 people.[22] An examination of floor plans in Pompeii shows typical atriums measuring 20' x 28'.[23] This would seat between 60 and 80 people.

The *ESV Study Bible* notes that early Christian churches "met in homes ... There is extensive archaeological evidence from many cites showing that some homes were structurally modified to hold such churches."[24] One such modified home known to host a church was found in Dura-Europos, Syria. It could, according to the archaeologists who excavated it, seat 65 to 70 people.[25] Jerome Murphy-O'Connor measured six homes in Pompcii and Ephesus and found the average atrium size to be 797 square feet.[26] This would seat around 100 people. Acts records 120 believers assembled in the upper room of a house.[27]

As first-century congregations grew, they did not erect bigger and bigger buildings. Instead, they multiplied, constantly training leaders and sending out groups to start new fellowships. Rather than growing your one congregation bigger and bigger, make it your goal to start new small

---

[21]"Lullingstone Roman Villa", English-Heritage.org.uk. Measurements taken from schematic.

[22]"Space Calculator for Banquet & Meeting Rooms", BanquetTablesPro.com, accessed October 04, 2016.

[23]William Smith, *A Dictionary of Greek and Roman Antiquities* (London: John Murray, 1875), 430.

[24]Lane Dennis, ed. *ESV Study Bible* (Wheaton, IL: Crossway Bibles, 2008), 2217

[25]Synder, 70. The impluvium had been tiled over and benches were added around the walls. Further, a wall had been removed between adjoining rooms creating a 714-square-foot area. A raised area was added at the front (for a podium?).

[26]Jerome Murphy-O'Connor, *Saint Paul's Corinth: Texts and Archaeology* (Collegeville, MN: Liturgical Press, 2002), 180.

[27]Acts 1:13, 15, 2:1-2.

churches that start other small churches.[28] Small churches align very much in size with apostolic churches that met in Roman villas.

PERSPECTIVE

There are both advantage and disadvantages to small churches. In the previous chapters, small churches were encouraged to play to their relational strengths by incorporating some of the practices of first-century house churches. In the West, the perceived disadvantages of small churches are mostly cultural. The Barna Group's study on why small churches don't grow revealed that people with children are often looking for a church that offers an impressive children's ministry, which in turn requires the funding for first-class facilities and to hire competent personnel, something smaller churches have financial difficulty doing.[29] How can this be overcome?

Many thriving small churches focus on reaching homeschool families. Those who have pulled their children out of both government and Christian schools are often not interested in their children being involved with Sunday school or youth groups. Impressive children's ministries mean little to them. One pastor of a church composed of homeschool families was asked if his church had a youth pastor; he replied it had not one but twenty youth pastors—each family's father.

A homeschool family's thinking is often based on such truths as, "Folly is bound up in the heart of a child" and "the companion of fools will suffer harm." [30] Because children are foolish, putting them all together in one class may be a recipe for spiritual and social disaster. The real influence in the room is not the teacher but peer pressure. Worst yet, many parents drop their children off at a church youth program as sort of a reform school, hoping for a miracle. The problem with this is the corrupting influence children have on each other: "Do not

---

[28]A helpful resource is *Becoming a Level Five Multiplying Church Field Guide* by Wilson & Ferguson (Exponential Resources, 2015).

[29]"Small Churches Struggle to Grow Because of the People They Attract," Barna. org, accessed September 01, 2016.

[30]Proverbs 22:15, 13:20.

be deceived: 'Bad company ruins good morals.'"[31] It is also felt that putting children in Sunday School or a youth group takes the pressure off the parents to fulfill their God-given roles of training their own children.

Barna's study found that singles under 35 were more open to attending small churches. This is good. However what happens when they marry and have children? Apart from homeschoolers, expect an exodus to a larger church with a first-rate children's program. What can be done? First, thank God for the years you had to make disciples of these Millennials before they moved on. Second, continue doing things to bring in new singles under 35. Some young couples who leave a small church upon having children will return after their children are grown. Someone needs to minister to singles and empty nesters, and small churches are in an excellent position to do so.

What constitutes a successful ministry anyway? How many people attend a church? How fast it grows? How big the budget is? Jesus went from 5000 down to 12 in one sermon.[32] Was Jesus' ministry a failure? *Of course not.* Noah faithfully preached to his generation, yet only a handful were saved. How successful was Isaiah's ministry to a dull, spiritually blind people?[33] He was successful because he was faithful to what God wanted him to do. Hence, a successful small church leader is one who is faithful to "preach the word; be ready in season and out of season; reprove, rebuke, and exhort, with complete patience and teaching."[34] It does not matter if your church never gets larger as long as one is faithful in God's household. The legacy of a faithful small church will outlast a larger, entertainment-oriented congregation. Let us strive to faithfully follow the example of Christ and the Apostles in our churches and ministries today.

If you lead your small church to adopt early church prac-tice, it will be a blessing to people. They will grow spiritually. It will likely create a contagious excitement that will cause

---

[31] 1 Corinthians 15:33.
[32] John 6:10, 24, 66-67.
[33] Isaiah 6:9-13.
[34] 2 Timothy 4:2.

numerical growth as well. We long to see the Lord's churches full if such growth represents people being reached with the Gospel and made into disciples. The temptation is to enjoy this growth, allowing the original church to get far larger than a typical church of the apostolic era. Instead of getting bigger and bigger, purpose to maintain the New Testament example of Roman-villa-sized churches. Build reproduction into the DNA of the church. Continually teach the men to be the leaders in their homes and the church. Train up new leaders from within. Once leadership is in place, send out a sizable portion of the original church to start new a small church.

Appendix D contains other practical considerations for small churches.

Go to NTRF.org for audio, articles, and a discussion guide on small church theology.

DISCUSSION QUESTIONS

1. What evidence is there that persecution was not the only reason the early church met in homes?

2. Some argue that Roman villa sized churches were characteristic of the church in its infancy, but not in its maturity. It was right and natural, they argue, for each church to grow beyond the confines of a home, building larger and larger places to meet. How do you feel about this?

3. Are we to believe that having smaller congregations was a purely incidental aspect of the blueprint for church life or was it purposeful? Why?

4. Why might the apostles have laid down a purposeful pattern of small churches?

5. What practical advantages and disadvantages would meeting in a home have?

6. What psychological impact might the size of a church meeting have on the actual meeting and people themselves?

7. How would the number of people involved impact a church's ability to have a participatory meeting or to achieve congregational consensus?

8. What advantages for growth and reproduction might house churches have over fellowships that have to build church houses?

9. What should be done in a situation where a home is simply too small to host a church meeting?

10. How did New Testament churches grow numerically yet still meet in private homes?

5

TIMELESS APOSTOLIC TRADITIONS

Why should doing church the first-century way matter to you? *Significant strengthening and enrichment await your fellowship through adopting the example given to us in the New Testament by the early church.* In view of the unique relationship between Jesus and His apostles, we should be very careful about neglecting the church practices they established.

PROFIT

Oxford University church history professor Stanley Greensdale stated: "The church exists to promote the worship of God, the inner life of the spirit, the evangelization of the world and the molding of society according to the will of God."[1] The premise is that the apostles knew the best methods to achieve these objectives and purposely patterned them for us in the churches they established. These should constitute normal and universal church practice. The LORD gave patterns and commands for the Tabernacle and worship under the Old Covenant. Did He fail to give patterns and commands for the Church and worship under the New Covenant? Adopting their ways better allow the Spirit to create love, unity, community, and commitment in a body of believers.

PRESUMPTION

Fee and Stuart, in the first edition of *How To Read The Bible For All Its Worth*, stated this about historical precedence: "Our assumption, along with many others, is that unless Scripture explicitly tells us we must do something, what is merely

---

[1] Stanley Lawrence Greensdale, "Early Christian Church," *Encyclopaedia Britannica*, ed. Warren Preece, Vol. 7 (Chicago: William Benton, Publisher, 1973), 844.

narrated or described can never function in a normative way."[2] No one, for example, would advocate following Jephthah's tragic example in Judges 11:29ff. The problem is that it is common for believers to also dismiss as optional the church practices described in the New Testament. It is presumed they were never intended to function as normal practice. What evidence is there the apostles might have intended their examples to be repeatable patterns?

PROOF #1—IT IS LOGICAL

It is logical—it just makes sense—to follow the church practice tradition of the apostles (as recorded in Scripture). If anyone truly understood the purpose of the church, surely it was the apostles. They were handpicked and personally trained by Jesus for three years. After His resurrection, our Lord appeared to them over a forty-day period.[3] Jesus then sent the Holy Spirit to teach them things He had not taught them.[4] Paul received a revelation of Jesus on the road to Damascus and then had further revelations in the wilderness plus the fourteen years following. The things Jesus taught these men about the church were naturally reflected in the way they set up and organized churches.

Paul boldly offered himself as an example to be followed with regard to his faithful service for Christ: "I urge you, then, be imitators of me. That is why I sent you Timothy ... to remind you of my ways in Christ, as I teach them everywhere in every church."[5] To also imitate Paul's ways in Christ regarding church practice would arguably be a wise choice for any fellowship.

Titus 1 deals directly with church practice. In verse 5, Paul wrote: "This is why I left you in Crete, so that you might put what remained into order, and appoint elders in every town as I directed you." It is evident from this passage that the apostles had a definite way they wanted certain things done regarding the church. It was not left up to each individual

---

[2]Gordon Fee & Douglas Stuart, *How To Read The Bible For All Its Worth*, 1st ed. (Grand Rapids, MI: Zondervan, 1982), 97.
[3]Acts 1:3.
[4]John 14-16.
[5]1 Corinthians 4:16-17.

assembly to find its own way. There was obviously some kind of order, pattern, or tradition that was followed in organizing the churches. Similarly, in 1 Corinthians 11:34 (a passage about the practice of the Lord's Supper), Paul wrote, "The rest I will **set in order** when I come" (KJV, italics mine). It is logical—it just makes sense—to prefer the church traditions of the apostles. If the apostles were to return and see how modern churches function, would they be pleased or grieved?

PROOF #2—IT IS PRAISEWORTHY

1 Corinthians 11 concerns church practice.[6] In 11:2, we see an apostle praising a church for holding to his *traditions* regarding worship: "I commend you because you remember me in everything and maintain the traditions even as I delivered them to you." The Greek for tradition, *paradosis*, means "that which is passed on."[7] This same Greek word (in verb form) was used in 1 Corinthians 11:23 with regard to the practice of the Lord's Supper (that it was passed on). Gordon Fee pointed out that *paradosis* in the context of 1 Corinthians 11 refers to religious traditions regarding worship.[8] The words "even as" in 11:2 indicate the degree of their compliance with these traditions: *exactly* as passed on to them.

It is noteworthy that the word "traditions" in 1 Corinthians 11:2 is plural. Paul had in mind more than the one tradition dealt with in 1 Corinthians 11a.[9] Mosaic legislation was paradigmatic in nature. It was case law. Only a few legal examples were recorded by Moses. The believer was expected to apply those case studies to other areas of life not specifically mentioned. Similarly, we argue that adherence to apostolic tradition is paradigmatic in nature. If we observe that the apostles were pleased when a church followed one specific tradition (such as in 1 Corinthians 11a), then we are expected to apply that approval to other patterns we see modeled

---

[6] For help with this topic, see "Women: Head Coverings," NTRF.org.

[7] Fritz Rienecker, Linguistic Key to the Greek New Testament (Grand Rapids: Zondervan Publishing House, 1980), p. 423. See also Beuer, Arndt, Gingrich & Danker, A Greek-English Lexicon of the New Testament (Chicago: University of Chicago Press, 1979), 615.

[8] Gordon Fee, *New International Commentary on the New Testament, The First Epistle to The Corinthians* (Grand Rapids: Wm. B. Eerdmans Publishing Co., 1987), 499.

[9] Fee, 500.

by the apostles in their establishment of churches. The Church, as the Bride of Christ, is too eternally important to allow her to go outside the patterns given by the Lord and His apostles. God's spiritual Temple must be built on the Chief Cornerstone both in doctrine and sound practice.

An interesting paradox can be observed about tradition *(paradosis)*. The same word used by Paul in 1 Corinthians 11:2 was also used by Jesus when He asked the Pharisees, "Why do you break the commandment of God for the sake of your tradition?"[10] Pharisaic tradition essentially broke God's commands. Whereas Jesus blasted the tradition of the Pharisees, Paul blessed the Corinthians for following his traditions. Apostolic tradition is consistent with the teachings of Christ. Holding to the traditions of the apostles is thus praiseworthy, as seen in Paul's praise for the Corinthian church (11:2).

PROOF #3—IT WAS UNIVERSAL

The churches of the New Testament universally followed apostolic traditions of church practice. 1 Corinthians 11 begins a four-chapter section on church practice. Paul quieted those who might disagree with these practices by appealing to the universal practice of all the other churches: "If anyone is inclined to be contentious, we have no such practice, nor do the churches of God" (1Co 11:16). This statement was designed to settle any objections. Paul expected all churches to do the same things. Prior emphasis had obviously been given to certain practices that were *supposed to be done the same way, everywhere.* Just to realize that one was different was argument enough to silence opposition. This indicates a uniformity of practice in all New Testament churches.

In 1 Corinthians 14:33b-35 (yet another passage about church practice), Paul mentioned something else that was true universally: "As in *all the churches* of the saints, the women should keep silent in the *churches*" (italics mine). Paul again appealed to a universal pattern that existed in all the churches as a basis for obedience.[11]

---

[10]Matthew 15:3.
[11]For help interpreting 1 Corinthians 14:33b-35, see "Women: Silent In Church" at NTRF.org.

All churches were expected to follow the same patterns for church meetings. The Corinthians were tempted to do things differently from all the other churches. Thus Paul chided them, "Or was it from you that the word of God came? Or are you the only ones it has reached?"[12] The obvious answer to both questions is **no**. These two questions were designed to keep the Corinthians in line with the practice of all the other churches. Holding to apostolic traditions (New Testament church patterns) was universal in the first century. Perhaps it should be today as well.

PROOF #4—IT BRINGS GOD'S PEACEFUL PRESENCE

The church at Philippi was told how to have the God of Peace be with them: "What you have learned and received and heard and seen in me—practice these things, and the God of peace will be with you."[13] The Philippians were instructed to put into practice what they 1) learned, 2) received, 3) heard from Paul, or 4) saw in Paul. The context concerned such things as imitating Christ's humility, putting others first, and rejoicing in the Lord. By extension could it not also include the way we see Paul organized churches? It is clear from Scripture how the apostles set up the early church. To bypass apostolic tradition in this area may be to bypass some of God's blessing. Could fellowships that follow apostolic *church* practice enjoy more of God's peaceful presence? Apostolic traditions for church practice include:

1. *Meeting weekly on Sunday, the Lord's Day, in honor of Jesus' resurrection.*

2. *Believer's baptism by immersion.*

3. *The separation of church and state.*

4. *Participatory worship services.*

5. *Celebrating the Lord's Supper weekly as a fellowship meal.*

6. *A plurality of co-equal elders leading every congregation.*

7. *The importance of building congregational consensus.*

8. *Roman villa-sized churches.*

[12] 1 Corinthians 14:36.
[13] Philippians 4:9.

Most churches follow some of these patterns, but not all. *Why not?* Perhaps it is because little attention is paid in seminary to the role apostolic traditions should play. Perhaps it is because most churches today are firmly entrenched in cultural church traditions developed long after the apostolic era. Many pastors have simply adopted historical traditions inherited from their denominations. Is there not a danger of neglecting the inspired tradition of the apostles for the sake of more modern tradition (Mt 15:1-3)?

We argue for consistency. The burden of explanation ought to fall on those who deviate from the New Testament pattern, not on those who desire to follow it. This consistency is especially important because the apostles evidently expected all churches to follow their traditions just as they were handed down (1Co 11:2). Perhaps these patterns of church practice are part of what gave the early church the dynamic that churches today are sometimes missing.

Proof #5—It Is Commanded

Although apostolic traditions make for interesting history, many think that following them is never commanded. However, 2 Thessalonians 2:15 instructs believers to "stand firm and hold to the traditions" (2Th 2:15).[14] It is not just apostolic *teachings* to which we should adhere, but also apostolic *traditions* (as revealed exclusively within the pages of Scripture).[15]

The overall context of 2 Thessalonians 2:15 refers to the apostles' teaching tradition of end-time events, not church practice *per se*. Yet again, the word "traditions" (2:15), is plural. The author had more traditions in view than merely the one teaching tradition about the second coming. Would it not also apply in principle to his traditions regarding church order, as patterned in the New Testament? We are to follow

---

[14]Imperative mode in Greek.

[15]Apostolic tradition, as recorded on the pages of the New Testament, is to be distinguished from the later historical tradition of the Catholic and Eastern churches.

the traditions of the apostles, not only in their theology, but also in their practice.[16]

PROFESSORS

Throughout church history, it has been common to view the church practices found in the New Testament as intended to set a biblical precedent. Though disagreeing with this view, Professors Fee and Stuart acknowledge that to most believers Acts "not only tell us the history of the early church, but it also serves as the normative model for the church of all times."[17] They go on to note: "almost all biblical Christians tend to treat precedent as having normative authority to some degree or another."[18] Both movements and denominations have been "founded partly on the premise that virtually all New Testament patterns should be restored as fully as possible in modern times ..."[19]

Early Southern Baptist theologian J. L. Dagg believed that the apostles "have taught us by example how to organize and govern churches. We have no right to reject their instruction and captiously insist that nothing but positive command shall bind us. Instead of choosing to walk in a way of our own devising, we should take pleasure to walk in the footsteps of those holy men from whom we have received the word of life ... respect for the Spirit by which they were led should induce us to prefer their modes of organization and government to such as our inferior wisdom might suggest."[20]

Roger Williams planted the first Baptist church in North America (1638). He believed churches should strive to follow as near as possible New Testament church forms and

---

[16]A similar attitude toward tradition is expressed in 2 Thessalonians 3:6-7a. Tradition here refers to practice more than doctrine. The apostles clearly wanted the churches to follow their traditions of <u>both</u> theology and practice. Should we limit those apostolic traditions that we follow *only* to eschatology and work habits?

[17]Fee & Stuart, 4th Ed., 112.

[18]Ibid, 125.

[19]Ibid, 130.

[20]J.L. Dagg, *Manual of Theology: A Treatise on Church Order* (Harrisonburg, VA: Gano Books, 1990), 84-86.

ordinances.[21] This belief led Williams to found the Rhode Island colony on the New Testament pattern of a separation between church and state.

According to E.H. Broadbent, church historian and undercover missionary to closed nations: "Events in the history of the churches in the time of the apostles have been selected and recorded in the Book of Acts in such a way as to provide a permanent pattern for the churches. Departure from this pattern has had disastrous consequences, and all revival and restoration have been due to some return to the pattern and principles in the Scriptures."[22]

Chinese church leader Watchman Nee said: "Acts is the 'genesis' of the church's history, and the Church in the time of Paul is the 'genesis' of the Spirit's work ... We must return to 'the beginning.' Only what God has set forth as our example in the beginning is the eternal Will of God. It is the Divine standard and our pattern for all time ... God has revealed His Will, not only by giving orders, but by having certain things done in His church, so that in the ages to come others might simply look at the pattern and know His will."[23]

It was missionary martyr Jim Elliot's firm conviction that "the pivot point hangs on whether or not God has revealed a universal pattern for the church in the New Testament. If He has not, then anything will do so long as it works. But I am convinced that nothing so dear to the heart of Christ as His Bride should be left without explicit instructions as to her corporate conduct ... it is incumbent upon me, if God has a pattern for the church, to find and establish that pattern, at all costs."[24]

A.W. Tozer wrote: "The temptation to introduce 'new' things into the work of God has always been too strong for some people to resist. The Church has suffered untold

---

[21]Edwin Gaustad, *Liberty of Conscience: Roger Williams In America* (Grand Rapids: Wm. B. Eerdmans Publishing Co.), 106.

[22]E.H. Broadbent, *The Pilgrim Church*, (Grand Rapids: Gospel Folio Press 1999), 26.

[23]Watchman Nee, *The Normal Christian Church Life* (Colorado Springs: International Students Press, 1969), 8-9.

[24]Elizabeth Elliot, *Shadow of The Almighty: Life and Testimony of Jim Elliot* (San Francisco, CA: Harper & Row, 1989), 138-139.

injury at the hands of well-intentioned but misguided persons, who have felt that they know more about running God's work, than Christ and His apostles did! A solid train of boxcars would not suffice to haul away the religious truck which has been brought into the service of the Church with the hope of improving on the original pattern. These things have been, one and all, great hindrances to the progress of the Truth, and have so altered the divinely planned structure that the apostles, were they to return to earth today, would scarcely recognize the misshapen thing which has resulted!"[25] He also concluded: "If the Holy Spirit was withdrawn from the church today, 95 percent of what we do would go on and no one would know the difference. If the Holy Spirit had been withdrawn from the New Testament church, 95 percent of what they did would stop, and everybody would know the difference."[26]

PROPOSITION

What can be concluded about God's interest in your church adhering to New Testament patterns for church practice? Remember Professors Fee and Stuart's presumption that what is merely narrated or described can never function in a normative way? In a later edition of their book they qualified their position somewhat: "Unless Scripture explicitly tells us we must do something, what is only narrated or described does not function in a normative (i.e. obligatory) way—*unless it can be demonstrated on other grounds that the author intended it to function in this way.*"[27] The purpose of this chapter is to demonstrate on other grounds that the apostles did indeed design for churches to follow the patterns they laid down for church order. Doing things their way is logical, praiseworthy, was universally practiced in first-century churches, brings God's peaceful presence, and is even commanded. The question is not *Must we do things the way they were done in the New Testament?*

---

[25]James Snyder, *Tozer On Worship And Entertainment* (Camp Hill, PA: Wind Hill Publisher, 1997), chapter 17.
[26]"A.W. Tozer on The Holy Spirit & Today's Church," Patheos.com. Accessed October 16, 2016.
[27]Ibid, 124.

Rather, the question is *Why would we want to do things any other way?*

PERSPECTIVE

Without Christ at the center of things, New Testament church life patterns become legalism and death, a hollow form, an empty shell (Jn 15:5). Even though all first-century churches adhered to apostolic practices they were still far from perfect, as seen in Jesus' words to the seven churches in Revelation. Adopting the ways of the apostles for church life are strategic stepping stones to put a fellowship in a better position to be all Christ wants it to be as His body. They will enrich your church but are not the answer to all its problems.

At the end of a very long life of faithful ministry, seminary professor L. Reginald Barnard cautioned that one can have a very scriptural idea of how the early church did things and yet miss the real idea of the church entirely.[28] Even if our church is identical to the apostolic ideal, we would have accomplished nothing unless that church was holier by far than the church we started with. Heaven forbid at the end we present a form to God, instead of a holy people redeemed by the Gospel.

We must always remember the church is people, the living body of Christ. Jesus died to sanctify His bride, presenting her to Himself without spot or wrinkle, holy and blameless. There is no perfect church. The church is the most relative thing God owns. Yet God will do His perfect work in His imperfect church, for it is His church.

When a church truly has spiritual wine, the best church practice wineskin for it is found in apostolic tradition. The church traditions of the apostles are simple, strategic, and scriptural. The most neglected practices are smaller congregations, participatory worship, the Lord's Supper celebrated weekly as a fellowship meal and elder-led congregational consensus. Incorporating these approaches into our

---

[28]L. Reginald Barnard, late professor of historical theology at Mid-America Baptist Theological Seminary, in letter to author, May 15, 1991.

churches today can result in tremendous blessing. Small churches have a bright future and tremendous potential if their leaders maintain a focus on disciple-making in the context of dynamic, Spirit-filled early church practice. It is a divine design!

See Appendix E for practical considerations on adopting timeless apostolic traditions.

Go to NTRF.org for an audio presentation and a leader's discussion guide on apostolic traditions.

Discussion Questions

1. How can the axiom *form follows function* be applied to how the apostles set up churches?

2. What in the New Testament indicates whether or not there was a basic uniformity of practice in all early churches?

3. Jesus criticized the Pharisees for holding to Jewish traditions (Mt 15). Yet Paul praised the Corinthians for holding to his traditions (1Co 11). Why the difference?

4. Why is it important to make a distinction between apostolic traditions found in the New Testament and later historical traditions?

5. Mosaic Law was paradigmatic in nature. How would the paradigmatic principle apply to commands in the New Testament to follow specific apostolic traditions (2Th 2:15, 3:6)?

6. What would give the apostles authority to establish patterns all churches are obliged to follow?

7. What is the difference between holding to apostolic traditions and mindlessly copying everything seen in the New Testament (wearing sandals, writing on parchment, studying by oil lamps, dressing in togas, etc.)?

8. Jesus washed His disciples' feet. The Jerusalem church practiced communalism. How can we determine what is and is not intended to be an apostolic tradition?

9. What should we make of the fact that there is scholarly consensus regarding the actual practice of the early church in the New Testament?

10. Some think it foolish to try to recreate the primitive church, because it was far from perfect. They assert that God expected His church to mature, to grow up, beyond the infancy stage. As much as anything, early believers are seen as examples of how **not** to function as a church. Besides, they argue, it is impossible to behave exactly like the first-century church because we no longer have the original apostles with us. How would you respond to this argument?

CONCLUSION

Jesus said: "No one pours new wine into old wineskins. If he does, the wine will burst the skins, and both the wine and the wineskins will be ruined. No, he pours new wine into new wineskins."[1] The simple point of Jesus' illustration is that some actions are inappropriate. If we were to compare the new wine to our lives together in Christ, then the wineskins could be likened to how we set up our churches (ecclesiology). Applying Jesus' words in principle, care must be taken not to organize our churches in ways that would be like unsuitable old wineskins. The best church structure is arguably found in the new wineskins of early church practice. Who knew better than the apostles how best to set up and order churches?

New Testament church dynamics are not all or nothing. Adopting even one could result in significant blessing for your church. Neither are they an end in and of themselves. They are merely stepping stones to help you accomplish the same new wine goals that are important to any Christ-honoring congregation, such as walking in the Spirit, love for the brethren, unity, evangelism, and disciple-making. The wine is much more important than the wineskin. Following the ways of the apostles will help create a church setting that makes the basics easier and more natural.

New Testament church practices were *simple*—a family atmosphere, prayer, weekly fellowship over food with friends who love Jesus and a commitment to the in-depth study of the apostles' teachings. In order to focus on the few New Testament essentials, it may be necessary to let go of common church programs. Economist E.F. Schumacher said, "Any intelligent fool can make things bigger and more complex. It takes a lot of genius and a lot of courage to move in the opposite direction."[2]

---

[1] Mark 2:22. After waiting patiently for Job's three friends to finish speaking, Elihu said, "Behold, my belly is like wine that has no vent; like new wineskins ready to burst. I must speak, that I may find relief; I must open my lips and answer" (Job 32:19-20).

[2] EF Schumacher, "Small is Beautiful", *The Radical Humanist* Vol. 37, No. 5 (August 1973), 22.

The ways of the early church were *strategic*—God's people got involved in church meetings through participatory worship, loving relationships were fostered in the weekly *Agapé* and the strong priority by the leaders to build congregational consensus promoted unity. Overflowing love and unity is a powerful witness to the watching world.

The church traditions of the apostles were *scriptural*—based on Jesus' teachings, clearly seen in the Bible, practiced by first-century believers and in some cases even prescribed by the New Testament.[3] They constituted a divine design for making disciples of all nations. Aren't they worthy of our consideration?

---

[3] 2 Thessalonians 2:15.

APPENDIX A

The Elements: One cup and one loaf should be visibly present to the congregation, symbolic of our unity in Christ. A pile of pre-broken crackers and pre-poured tiny cups pictures individualism and disunity. The entire congregation should partake of the one cup and one loaf. Anglicans have done this for centuries without obvious harm to their health.[1] Another option is to pour from one large decanter into smaller cups, or to dip one's bread into the common cup.

Starting Out: Church planters can easily make the weekly celebration of the Holy Meal an integral part of the Sunday meetings from the church's inception. Existing churches might consider beginning with a gradual phase-in of the Lord's Supper as a weekly fellowship meal. Perhaps make the meal optional at first; serve the elements as usual followed by a meal in the fellowship hall for those who wish to participate. Go slowly. Allow people to get excited about it and tell others. Moreover, unless people are thoroughly persuaded of the Scriptural basis for celebrating the Lord's Supper weekly as a fellowship meal, there will be resistance to having to go to the trouble to prepare and bring food each week. Be sure people understand the holy nature of the meal. It is not just an inconvenient lunch. It is a sacred, covenant meal before the Lord with His children.

The Weakness of Wednesday-Night Suppers: Many churches offer a Wednesday-night fellowship meal. Although it may be good to introduce the Lord's Supper as a meal in conjunction with the existing Wednesday-night meal, this should be seen merely as a transitional step. Two thousand years of Christian history in the West have rightly ingrained into believers the notion that what happens on Sundays is what is really important. As the Lord's Supper/*Agapé* was the main reason the early church gathered each Lord's Day, the goal should be to celebrate it each Sunday, giving it the same prominence the apostles gave it. Grace

---

[1] Perhaps this is because Anglicans use wine, which kills the germs.

unto unity comes as the entire congregation partakes of the cup and loaf, not just the minority who come on Wednesday night. The entire congregation needs to experience the weekly fellowship of the *Agapé*.

Integration: The bread and wine were given in the context of an actual dinner. Be careful not to separate the elements from the meal too much, as if the Lord's Supper is the cup and loaf and everything else is just lunch. First, get the meal completely ready and then distribute the elements to mark the beginning of the meal. One approach is to point out the significance of the elements and lead in prayer as usual. Then, ask all the heads of each household to come up and take the elements back for their families. As each family finishes, they can go ahead through the serving line to enjoy the banquet aspect of the holy meal. This is a freedom issue; do what works best for your church.

Leaven: Should the bread be unleavened and the fruit of the vine alcoholic? The Jews ate unleavened bread in the Passover to symbolize the quickness with which God brought them out of Egypt. No doubt Jesus used unleavened bread in the original Last Supper. However, nothing is said in the New Testament about Gentile churches using unleavened bread in the Lord's Supper. Though sometimes in the New Testament yeast is associated with evil (1Co 5:6-8), it is also used to represent God's kingdom (Mt 13:33). The real symbolism lies with the bread as a representation of Jesus' body, leavened or not.

Regarding the cup, it is clear from 1 Corinthians 11 that actual wine was used in the Lord's Supper, because some had become drunk. However, no clear theological reason is ever given in the New Testament for it being alcoholic (but consider Genesis 27:28, Isaiah 25:6-9, and Romans 14:21). Jesus simply called it the fruit of the vine. The object lesson is that red wine looks like blood. As with leavened or unleavened bread, the use of wine or grape juice would seem to be a matter of freedom for each local church to decide with spiritual sensitivity for one another.

Unbelievers: Most churches restrict access to the elements in some way. For example, the *Baptist Faith and Message* of 2000 holds baptism to be the prerequisite for the privileges of the Lord's Supper. Celebrating the Lord's Supper as it was celebrated in the New Testament as a full meal may change one's perspective somewhat on the presence of unbelievers. By all means, point out that the bread and wine are for believers only. The Lord's Supper, as a sacred, covenant meal, has significance only to believers. Yet, to nonbelievers present, it is merely another meal. Unbelieving adults and our own children too young to believe get hungry just like believers do; invite them to enjoy the feast along with you. Love them to the Lord! The danger in taking the Lord's Supper in an unworthy manner applies only to believers (1Co 11:27-32). In short, elements no, meal yes.

Where Did It Go? It appears that from the mid-third century onward, the bread and wine of the Lord's Supper were separated from the meal. However, even though the two were separated, the church continued to practice both until sometime after Constantine (who died in A.D. 337). Eventually, the love feast fizzled completely out. Perhaps it would have continued on down to the present had the original apostolic tradition of keeping the two together not been broken. Then, during the Protestant Reformation, the central altar so prominent in Catholicism was replaced by the pulpit and the centrality of the preached Word. Thus, in many Protestant churches, the weekly observance of communion was discontinued.

Eusebius, as bishop, consecrated a church building in Tyre. In the dedication, he praised the most holy altar as the center of the building. Then, in the late 300s, the Synod of Laodicea forbade the celebration of the Lord's Supper in houses. Davids and Grossman offer this comment, "Once you have an altar with 'holy food', mixing it with the common food of a communal meal appears profane. Thus the focus on the table as altar brings about the forbidding of celebrating the Lord's Supper in houses. The irony is that in the tabernacle and temple the central act of worship was a family meal in the presence of the deity, the temple being part slaughterhouse and part bar-b-que, as well as being the place where animal fat was burned and incense was offered."[2]

---

[2]Peter Davids and Siegfried Grossmann, "The Church in the House," paper, 1982.

Logistics: Sandra Atkerson offers the following practical ideas on logistics: "Ask each family to prepare food at home and bring it to share with everyone else. Many churches have had great success with the pot luck (or pot providence) method. The Lord's Supper is a feast of good and bountiful food with fellowship centered around Christ, a picture of the marriage banquet of the Lamb. It is a time to give and share liberally with our brothers and sisters in Christ. As for how much to bring, if you were having one more family over for dinner with your family, how much of one dish would you prepare? If church were cancelled for some reason, could you satisfy your own family with what you prepared to take to the Lord's Supper? Encourage each family to bring a main dish and a side dish. Desserts should be considered optional and brought as a third dish but never as the only dish by a family. At least enough food should be brought by every family to feed themselves and have more left over to share with others. The singles, especially those not inclined to cook, might bring drinks, peanuts, dessert, chips and dip, or a prepared deli item such as potato salad or rotisserie chicken. The congregation should see this as a giving expense, a ministry, an offering to the Lord.

Confusion is minimized at the time of serving if your dish is ready when you arrive. Cook it before you come. Consider investing in a Pyrex Portables insulated hot/cold carrier that will keep your food at the temperature at which it was prepared. Hot plates can be plugged in to keep dishes warm. Others could bring crock pots. The oven can be put on warm and dishes stored there. Wool blankets or beach towels work well for hot/cold insulation during transport. Coolers in the summer months are great for icing down cold dishes.

The main point to remember for food safety is to keep hot foods hot at 150 degrees and cold foods cold at 40 degrees. Once the food is out for serving, it should sit out no longer than 2-3 hours before it is refrigerated. Dispose of any food left out longer than four hours.

Parents should consider helping their children prepare plates. Little ones often have eyes bigger than their stomachs and much food can go to waste. Many churches prefer to buy smaller 12 or 16 ounce cups. Most folks tend to fill their cups full, often not drinking it all. Smaller cups make less waste. It is better to go back for refills than to throw away unwanted drink.

A word about hygiene might be appropriate—there can never be enough hand washing among friends! Be sensitive to germs. All folks going through the serving line should wash before touching serving utensils. Put out a pump jar of hand sanitizer right by the plates at the beginning of the line. To help with cleanup, consider using paper plates and plastic cups and forks."

The Lord's Prayer: Feasting at Christ's coming may also be reflected in the Lord's Prayer. Immediately after "Thy kingdom come" is "Give us each day our daily bread" (Lk 11:2-3). The Greek here is difficult; it reads something like, "the bread of us belonging to the coming day give us today" (the ESV marginal note reads, "bread for tomorrow"). Tomorrow's bread today? Jesus may have been teaching us to ask that the bread of the coming kingdom banquet be given to us today: "Let your kingdom come—Let the feast begin today!" Renowned theologian Athanasius of Alexandria explained it as "the bread of the world to come."[3]

---

[3]Frederick Godet, *Commentary on Luke* (Grand Rapids, MI: Kregel Publications, 1981), 314.

Appendix B

Leadership's Role: Lexicographer Joseph Thayer defined an *episcopos* as "a man charged with the duty of seeing that things to be done by others are done rightly."[1] He described a *presbutéros* as one who "presided over the assemblies".[2] Church leaders new to the idea of participatory worship are wisely cautious. With good reason, they anticipate unedifying scenarios. One of an elder's roles is to keep things on track, in order and true to the prime directive that all things be edifying. If what goes on in a meeting is not edifying, the elders, more than anyone, else are responsible for making it right.

Ephesians 4:11-12 reveals it is the duty of pastor-teachers to equip the saints for ministry. This includes training the saints so they are equipped to contribute meaningfully in a participatory meeting. If the Scriptures truly reveal God's desire for participatory meetings, then we can expect God to work through the elders to see to it that the meetings will be successful in the long run. While there is order in a cemetery, there is no life. It is much better to have life and risk a little disorder. The Holy Spirit must be trusted to work in the life of a church.

Edifying participatory church meetings do not just happen. Although New Testament styled participatory worship is to be Spirit-led, the Spirit uses elders to help make it edifying. They are behind-the-scene coaches, encouraging and training so that everyone operates from out of his spiritual gift and everything said and done is edifying. Below are some typical scenarios to be expected. These are detailed in the hope that those just beginning to experiment with participatory meetings can avoid some of the more common pitfalls.

Baby Steps: Start slowly. Don't try to have fully participatory meetings all at once. All during the week, when you hear a brother sharing about something the Lord has

---

[1] Joseph Thayer, *Greek-English Lexicon of the New Testament* (Grand Rapids, MI: Baker Book House, 1977), 243.
[2] Ibid, 536.

taught him, ask him to give a short (7 minutes or less) sharing about it on the next Sunday in church. Work with him to make sure it is short and application oriented. Coach him to be sure the point is clear.

A person who tells about a witnessing experience can serve to motivate the more timid to evangelism. A testimony about answered prayer or a need met in God's timing and providence can encourage others going through hard times. A person involved in a jail ministry can tell about good results among inmates and induce others to get involved. Real-life stories—with a spiritual emphasis—are tremendously uplifting. Each week, schedule a few brothers in advance to share something short in the meeting. This will get the congregation accustomed to more participation and model the type of sharing that is expected and edifying. As the congregation grows accustomed to it, the time allotted for sharing can increase and more liberty extended to those moved by the Spirit to get up and share without having been scheduled.

Cultural Resistance: It is counter-cultural in the West to have participatory worship instead of performance styled worship led from the front. Many will find participatory worship uncomfortable. One Baptist church that experimented with participatory worship Sunday nights suffered a dramatic decline in attendance at that service. (People said that they did not want to hear amateurs' opinions; they wanted to hear polished presentations by professional pastors). It takes time, teaching, training and equipping by the leadership to ready God's people for participatory worship. The typical church member is a not professional speaker and the potential is always there for imperfect presentations. However, "love bears all things" (1Co 13:7). If participatory worship is truly Christ's desire, then it does not matter how strange it seems in our culture. Like the pearl of great price, the benefit is worth the cost. People will become more open to participatory meetings as they are taught obedience to God's Word and understand that it is a scriptural concept.

Pew Potatoes: Most Christians, after years of passively

attending services, are conditioned to sit silently in church as if watching television. It takes encouragement and patience to overcome this. Meaningful participation will seem awkward to people at first. Continual prompting and encouraging by the leadership may be necessary until the sound barrier is broken. Elders should work behind the scenes during the week encouraging the brethren to share. Asking various men to lead in a weekly prayer or public reading of Scripture can help them to overcome being timid.

Open participation does not preclude prior private preparation. Every brother should be coached to consider *in advance* how the Lord might have him to edify the church.[3] If a string were stretched across a stream at water level, various things would become attached to it as the day passed, things that otherwise would have floated on past. Similarly, thinking all week long about what to bring to the next meeting helps greatly. If no one brought food to a family reunion, there would not be much of a feast. If no one comes to participatory worship prepared to contribute, there will not be much sharing.

Ask the brothers, *What has the Lord shown you this week in your time with Him? Is there a testimony the Lord would have you to bring? Could you purpose to begin a time of conversational prayer? Is there a song that would edify the church? Is there some subject or passage of Scripture to teach on?*

The worse cause for lack of participation is a lack of anything spiritual to share. Many Christians are not walking with the Lord and not living Spirit-filled lives. They may be as straight as a gun barrel theologically, but just as empty. Such spiritually dull believers will have little worthwhile to share on Sunday. Worst yet, if they do get up to speak, it will likely cause vexation. Edifying participatory worship only happens when church members are abiding in Jesus. Too often, liturgy and dominance by clergy become a necessary cover for congregational carnality. On the other hand, genuine heartfelt sharing and confession in the meeting can cause those living lives of hypocrisy to come under

---

[3]Hebrews 10:25.

conviction and repent of their sin. Obedience is contagious! People who love Jesus do not come to church to worship; they bring their worship with them.

Unedifying Remarks: Sometimes, after brothers start sharing, they get too casual. Unless gifted in prophecy, things said spontaneously off the top of the head typically don't edify the assembly. Just because it is an open meeting does not mean people can say anything they want to say. Leaders need to remind the church that anything said in the meeting must be designed to build up the body and to encourage everyone else. Sometimes, merely requiring speakers to rise and stand behind a pulpit, lectern, or music stand at the front will effectively squelch unedifying casual remarks. The elders must coach each person to remember Proverbs 25:11, "A word fitly spoken is like apples of gold in a setting of silver."

Church meetings must not become therapy sessions for the wounded, with everything focused on needy persons. If allowed to do so, spiritual black holes can suck the life out of the meeting. Though such people do need counseling, it should be done at a time other than during public worship. Edification is the prime directive.

It is the elders' responsibility to help people understand what is and is not edifying and to coach people in private about making only edifying comments. Brothers should be trained to tell what time it is, not how to build a clock. Like a pencil, every message should have a point. Those who share should also be taught to keep it down to only one point. The words spoken must have a punch, an exhortation. Despite the best modeling, some brothers simply will not "get it"; they will have to be privately and repeatedly coached as to what comments are and are not edifying.

There is to be a certain degree of decorum. As Peter said, "As each has received a gift, use it to serve one another, as good stewards of God's varied grace: whoever speaks, as one who speaks oracles of God" (1Pe 4:10-11). Participatory worship should not be interactive. It is generally not edifying when someone in the audience tries to interact with the person who was burdened to get up and share. The church should not be subjected to having to listen to a public conversation. During the worship time, people should present verbal offerings to edify the church with the same attitude that Old Testament saints brought offerings. Discourage others from piling on or adding to something that has already been offered (we call it diescling).

Aberrant Theology: The lure of a participatory meeting may draw in those looking to promote some eccentric doctrine. This again is where elders are needed. Timothy, temporarily functioning as an elder, was to "charge certain persons not to teach any different doctrine" (1Ti 1:3). Scripture also tells us that one qualification for an elder is that he must "be able to give instruction in sound doctrine and also to rebuke those who contradict it" (Tit 1:9). Similarly, Titus was told to "exhort and rebuke with all authority. Let no one disregard you" (Tit 2:15). John warned about a known deceiver: "do not receive him into your house" (2Jn 1:10).[4] The prevention and correction of error is one reason elders are needed.

One way to filter out those promoting doctrinal error is for the church to have an official statement of faith. Anything said in the church meeting must be consistent with the belief statement. In addition, only allow brothers to speak who are intimately involved with and in good standing with the church (not those who have not joined the church). Those with non-heretical but just plain odd beliefs must not be free to publicly express these either. The elders are gates through which would-be speakers must pass.

Pooled Ignorance: A Christian radio broadcaster, during an interview on participatory worship, astutely asked, "How do you keep the guy who knows the least from saying the most?" Rather than considering in advance how to encourage the church, some will come to the meeting totally unprepared. Socially clueless and without the Spirit's leading, they will make impromptu, rambling speeches that would be better left unsaid. It is the elders' job to know the congregation so well that they know who is likely to do excessive and inappropriate sharing. They must work with him to be informed, concise, and judicious in how often he speaks.

---

[4] John's instructions were especially relevant in churches with participatory meetings.

Disruptive Visitors: Uninformed guests could easily vex the church with unedifying remarks. Socially clueless or self-centered visitors may want to dominate the meeting. The mentally unstable will seek to speak loudly and often, to the chagrin of the assembly. Critics might publically attack what the church believes. Traveling heretics will view the participatory meeting as a chance to promote errant theology. Leaders are needed in such cases to keep the peace and restore order with wisdom and patience. Since an ounce of prevention is worth a pound of cure, it would be wise to allow only church members or invited guests the opportunity to speak. God's flock must be protected from unnecessary vexation.

Congregational Size: Meetings that are either too big (hundreds) or too small (less than thirty) create their own set of hindrances to participatory gatherings. Too many people present will intimidate the shy and work against open sharing, accountability, and intimacy. Only a tiny fraction of those present in a big meeting would be able to share anyway (even if they had the nerve). Too few people and the meeting can seem dull; diversity of spiritual gifts will be lacking. The typical first-century church, meeting in a wealthy person's villa, would hold some 65-70 people.[5] There were 120 in the upper room.[6] Early church meetings were made up of scores of people, not hundreds upon hundreds and certainly not thousands.

Latecomers: Suppose a brother is earnestly sharing something from his heart when suddenly in bursts a family arriving late. All eyes will naturally turn to see who is entering. As they climb over people already seated and chairs are shuffled and coats removed, what impact do you suppose it will have on the message that was being shared? It will be disrupted and the Spirit squelched. Ask those arriving late to wait quietly outside, not entering the meeting area until a song is being sung or there has been a break in the speaking.

It has frequently happened in participatory worship that a person arriving late will request a song that has already

---

[5]Graydon Synder, *Church Life Before Constantine* (Macon, GA: Mercer University Press, 1991), 70.

[6]Acts 1:15 may not reflect a normal church meeting, but it does show how many could assemble in a first century room.

been sung. Worse yet, a late brother will bring an exhortation relative to some current event that the church already spent ten minutes considering before he arrived. The church might adopt a policy asking anyone coming late to refrain from speaking in that meeting, as he would have no idea what transpired prior to his arrival.

So Little Time: If you are limited to a one-hour service, it will be difficult to pack in music, participatory sharing, and an in-depth lesson. You will have to carefully watch the time designed for each phase of the meeting (singing, sharing, teaching), limit the number who can share, and shorten the time allotted to each. A limit of 7 to 10 minutes might be put on anything said. This will help keep any one person from dominating the meeting and free up air time for multiple people to share. It will be necessary for the leadership to occasionally interrupt long-winded speakers after the 10-minute mark is passed. A one-and-a-half or two-hour meeting would be more ideal but, even then, the clock must be carefully watched. A sample schedule/bulletin is at the end of this appendix.

In-Depth Teachings: Feeding the sheep is a critical component of healthy church life. Quality, in-depth teaching that is geared toward believers should be an integral part of each Sunday church meeting. This is the "lesson" listed in 1 Corinthians 14:26. Our Lord instructed the apostles to make disciples by *teaching* them to obey everything He commanded (Mt 28:20). We learn from Acts 2:42 that the Jerusalem church was devoted to the apostles' *teaching*. One of the requirements of an elder is that he be able to *teach* (1 Ti 3:2). Elders who work hard at *teaching* are declared worthy of double honor (financial support, 1 Ti 5:17-18). All this taken together demands an appreciation for the importance of teaching. The ideal is a steady diet of the systematic exposition of Scripture with clear, practical applications. (If the "what"—the content—does not lead to the "so what"—the application—then the "what" has not been taught correctly). The goal of all instruction should be love from a pure heart, a good conscience, and a sincere faith (1 Ti 1:5). Because we want to see people come to Christ, it can be tempting to turn church meetings into evangelistic services. Though unbelievers may regularly attend worship services, the New Testament indicates church gatherings are primarily for the benefit of believers, to build Christians up in their faith and encourage them to obedience.

In the weekly teaching time, consider teaching through books of the Bible, paragraph by paragraph, bringing out the main point the inspired author made and appropriately applying it to your congregation (expository teaching). Many pastors feel their teaching to be expository teaching even though they feed the sheep a steady diet of topical sermons. There is a place for topical messages created by piecing together verses from all over the Bible, but a steady diet of this is not healthy. Expository teaching is systematically teaching through the various books of the Bible. Carefully develop the successive topics found within each book. Yet, be aware that creating a sermon out of every word in a verse is not expository teaching—it is a series of topical sermons using the pretense of teaching through a Bible book. Cover enough of the text each week to bring out the inspired author's original concern, illustrate that intent, and motivate your congregation to obey it in their present context.

One celebrity preacher called teaching from the Bible easy and cheating. He even claimed people don't grow that way (!). Instead, he serves his massive congregation witty, entertaining, topical messages drawn almost entirely from his own imagination. Our view is that while our own ideas and notions may be brilliant and entertaining, what ultimately matters is what the Holy Spirit inspired the biblical author to write. In the final analysis, people don't need to hear what you or I think about things. Instead, teach the Word of God.

Three Phases: We recommend three phases to every Lord's Day meeting. The first phase might be participatory sharing and worship, followed by a short break. The second phase could be the lesson brought by a brother qualified to teach, followed by a break. The third phase would be the Lord's Supper/*Agapé*. Of course, the order of the phases could be rearranged as best meets the needs of the fellowship.

Sample Bulletin:

Our Gathering Together

10:15 – 10:30 ~ Arrive & Settle In

▶ Meet people, enjoy a cup of coffee and find a seat.

10:30 – 11:15 ~ Participatory Worship

▶ First-century church meetings were charactcrized by "each one has" (1Co 14:26). Accordingly, brothers in good standing with the church are free to use their spiritual gifts to build up the gathered saints through song, short testimony, Scripture reading, exhortation, or praise.

11:15 – 11:30 ~ Short Break

▶ Stand up, stretch your legs, refresh your coffee, and greet someone.

11:30 – 12:15 ~ Lesson

▶ An integral part of our participatory worship is the in-depth teaching of God's Word, brought by an elder or brother with the gift of teaching.

12:30 – 2:30 ~ Lords' Supper / Agapé Feast

▶ The early church celebrated the Lord's Supper weekly as an actual meal. This holy meal is a wonderful time of edification through fellowship. Central to all is the bread and wine, symbolizing Jesus' death on the cross to pay for our sins. The one cup and one loaf symbolize unity. Like an enacted prayer, reminds of His promise to come back and eat it again with us at the Wedding Banquet of the Lamb.

Come, Lord Jesus!

Charismatic Gifts: Churches that practice charismatic gifts must be sure the guidelines of 1 Corinthians 14:26-32 are followed closely. Tongues are not to be allowed unless interpreted. There is to be a limit of three who speak in tongues. Only one at a time should speak. Prophecies are also to be limited to three speakers. Anyone who prophesies must realize that his words will be weighed carefully and judged. Dealing with this can be messy and frustrating since the overly emotional and unstable often imagine they have such gifts. Perhaps that is why the Thessalonians had to be told, "do not treat prophecies with contempt. Test everything. Hold on to the good. Avoid every kind of evil" (1Th 5:20-22). In the midst of these supernatural utterances, there must be order: "The spirits of the prophets are subject to the control of the prophets. God is not a God of disorder but of peace" (1Co 14:33a). Here again, elders play a key role in helping everything that goes on to be done in a "fitting and orderly way" (1Co 14:40). The elders are the quality control men.

Women: Participatory worship obviously does not mean anything goes. Everything said has to edify the church. There are limits on how many could speak in tongues or prophesy. Only one at a time can speak. Tongues-speakers must be silent if there is no interpreter; prophets must be silent if interrupted. In each case there is to be a holding back for the greater good. As 1 Timothy 2:12 reveals that women are not to teach or have authority over men, sisters are not free to bring the lesson mentioned in 1 Corinthians 14:26. Further, 1 Corinthians 14:33b-35 appears to further limit the sisters' participation in some way. It appears the sisters are to refrain from using their verbal gifts in the plenary church meeting. Perhaps it is a dynamic silence—a purposeful holding back—so as to encourage the men to lead out. (Articles on this topic can be found at NTRF.org).[7]

Children: The New Testament indicates that children were present with their parents in the meeting. For example,

---

[7]"Women: Silent in Church?"

Paul intended some of his letters to be read aloud to the entire church (Col 4:16); had children not been present in the meeting they would not have heard Paul's instruction to them (Ep 6:1-3; see also Mt 19:13-15, Lk 2:41-50, Acts 21:5). It is generally best for children to remain with their parents in worship, rather than being segregated in a children's church.

A very young child who begins crying loudly in the meeting should be removed from the meeting by a parent until he is quieted. It is good to have a dedicated room to go to for this purpose. Some parents will be oblivious to this need and, in such cases, the leadership must speak to the parents in private to enlist their cooperation in controlling their children. Older children should be taught to sit still or play silently on the floor so as not to disrupt the meeting.

False Expectations: Some new people will invariably come to participatory worship with preconceived notions of what the meeting should be like. Some, for instance, will want a moving worship experience or to sing only the great hymns of the faith. Others will exclusively associate praise songs with heartfelt worship, or expect dramatic healings to take place, or want some emotional presentation of the Gospel. When their expectations are not met, disappointment and discontentment are the result. Church leaders need to be aware of this and take steps to help people to have biblical expectations of the meetings and to have the same goals that our Lord does. To help overcome false expectations, a description of a typical church meeting could be posted on the church website, a brief statement made in each service about how the church meeting will be conducted and a bulletin handed to visitors stating what to expect:

Regenerate Membership: The ability to follow the small church practices read about in the New Testament assumes a regenerate church membership. The Reformers felt one of the marks of a true church was church discipline.[8] The wonder of the Gospel is that provision is made for the sinning brother who cannot find his own way to repentance: the good graces of a loving congregation will help him be restored to

---

[8]*Belgic Confession*, Article 29.

full fellowship.[9] Consider the following principles from a full article at NTRF.org:

1. *The motivation for all discipline is the love of the Father.*

2. *Most discipline is private and personal.*

3. *Most discipline is accomplished through study of the Word and prayer and the active work of the Holy Spirit in a believer's life.*

4. *The practice of sin is a church family issue and sometimes must be dealt with by other members of the family for the sake of both the brother and the family.*

5. *God Himself is the one who exposes and brings all things to light.*

6. *All spiritually mature members of the body are called to this body ministry.*

7. *Prayer and self-examination are required before confronting someone.*

8. *Be careful to protect the sinning brother's privacy by going to him in private.*

9. *If the brother rejects the counsel, go to him with two or three witnesses.*

10. *"If he refuses to listen to them, tell it to the church."*

11. *"If he refuses to listen even to the church, let him be to you as a Gentile and a tax collector."*

---

[9]Matthew 18:15-22.

APPENDIX C

Consensus or Simple Majority? Should decisions be made by *consensus* or *simple majority?* Consider what is implied in those two options. The word consensus means general agreement, representative trend, or opinion. It is related to the words "consent" and "consensual." In contrast, majority rule can be a 51% dictatorship for the 49% who don't agree and this certainly works against unity. Consensus, however, seeks to build unity.

Would God have His church make decisions based on consensus or majority rule? Consider the following biblical texts: "How good and pleasant it is when brothers live together in unity" (Ps 133:1); "I appeal to you, brothers, in the name of our Lord Jesus Christ, that all of you agree with one another so that there may be no divisions among you and that you may be perfectly united in mind and thought" (1Co 1:10); "Make every effort to keep the unity of the Spirit through the bond of peace" (Ep 4:3); "Make my joy complete by being like-minded, having the same love, being one in spirit and purpose" (Php 2:2); "Clothe yourselves with compassion, kindness, humility, gentleness and patience. Bear with each other and forgive whatever grievances you may have against one another. Forgive as the Lord forgave you. And over all these virtues put on love, which binds them all together in perfect unity" (Col 3:12-15).

Systematic, thoroughly thought out, well-presented teaching that is soaked in fervent prayer on any given matter under discussion will facilitate mature discussion. Even though leaders will bring teachings during church meetings that are relevant to the issue under consideration, much of the consensus building process will occur apart from a church service. It will happen one-on-one, brother to brother, during the fellowship of the Lord's Supper, in midweek social visits, via phone conversations, by text and e-mail, etc. To bring church members into agreement with one another takes time, patience, humility, gentleness and the ministry of elders.

There is a vast difference between consensus and simple majority rule (which involves voting and a 51% "win").

Congregational Voting: In the consensus process, there may never be a time that an actual vote is taken on anything. The leadership should know each brother's position based on having spoken to each one individually. In this process, due consideration should be given to the opinions of godly, mature, longstanding members rather than those who just begin to attend. When the time is right, after overall consensus is reached, after any remaining few dissenters have been asked to yield to the elders, the achievement of consensus can be announced and the proposal implemented.

Should there be a general meeting of the church where an issue is discussed to find out if there is consensus? Ideally, the church should be small enough that the leadership knows where each person in the church stands on any given issue without necessarily having to call a general meeting. However, it would be appropriate to have special meetings (apart from worship services) for teaching and discussing important issues.

How does male leadership in the home and church impact this process? Men who are weak leaders in the home will be weak leaders in the church. Involving all the brothers in the consensus process will help strengthen the men of the church and encourage them to be better leaders at home.

In the consensus process, exactly who makes the decisions, men and women both or only the men? *See 1 Corinthians 11:1ff, 14:33-35, 1 Timothy 2:11-15.* Everyone's thoughts are important. Within the Trinity, though God the Father and God the Son are equal persons, the Son voluntarily submits to the Father's will. Even though men and women are absolutely equal in God's sight, wives are called on to submit to their husbands. God is the head of Christ, Christ is the head of the church, and the husband is the head of his family. One way this order is expressed within the church is that only men are to serve as elders and teachers. This order is further expressed in that the men, as the heads of their homes, are ultimately to represent their wives' opinions in the consensus process. Certainly, the wives have valid opinions and insights. These concerns may be expressed directly by the women or through their husbands. A loving husband will duly consider his wife's views, but it is the brothers who have the last say. It is the brothers who must make decisions that are binding on the church.

In matters of mere preference, being considerate of the women and yielding to their desires is the proper course to take. However, in matters of theology or the application of theological or sin issues, the men must make the final decisions. In his commentary on 1 Corinthians 14:33-35, R.C.H. Lenski quotes from an *Opinion of the Theological Faculty of Capital University*: "How the granting of voice and vote to women in all congregational meetings can do anything but place women completely on a level with men in all such meetings and gravely interfere with their divinely ordered subjection and obedience, we are unable to see."[1]

When do issues rise to the level that church consensus is needed? It is impractical to involve the church in every little decision that is made. The key is to focus on consensus in major issues: how funds are spent, elder and deacon selection, where the church meets, big changes to the way meetings are conducted, planting a new church, sending or supporting missionaries, starting outreach ministries, etc.

When does the size of the congregation become a problem? No magic number is ever given in Scripture. If a church is too big for the elders to know and have a relationship with every man, it is too big. Consensus governing works best in a congregation small enough for everyone to know and love each other. Relationships must be strong enough to allow people to work through disagreements without someone getting upset and leaving the church. It is noteworthy that the early church met in Roman villas; the typical villa could accommodate around 100 people.

What about the uncommitted or newly converted— Do their voices count in the consensus process? There

---

[1] RCH Lenski, *The Interpretation of I and II Corinthians* (Minneapolis: Augsburg Publishing House, 1943), 617.

will almost always be spiritually immature people in a church. Their opinions should carry as much weight as their involvement with the church. This is also precisely where Hebrews 13:17 comes into play. After reasonable discussion and appeal, such persons are to listen to and yield to the wisdom of the elders.

How should universal church consensus apply to interpreting the Bible? Certainly, we should study the Bible as individuals, but we should not study the Bible individualistically. We need to weigh our interpretations against the consensus of the whole Church—not just our local church, but the Church universal. Historical humility is called for. To reject the time-tested conclusions of millions of our fellow believers over thousands of years is to effectively make one's self into a little Pope (who fancies he has divine right to interpret Scripture on his own).[2]

The Scriptures teach that the Holy Spirit dwells in every believer. As we survey the beliefs of the Church around the world today and throughout the past two millennia of church history, various fundamental agreements can be readily observed concerning the correct interpretation of Scripture. This has to be more than coincidence. It is the work of the Spirit. Some of these general agreements are about such matters as the virgin birth, the Trinity (One God in Three Persons), the deity of Christ, the propitiatory nature of Christ's death on the cross, the bodily resurrection of Christ, the future bodily return of Christ, the future bodily resurrection of the dead, and the inspiration of Scripture. When the entire church universal has arrived at a consensus regarding a doctrine, it becomes authoritative. Does one lone congregation have the right to defy the consensus of the whole church in the world and throughout history? These basic agreed-upon doctrines constitute the *regula fide*, the rule of faith. We need a good dose of historical humility!

Thus, we see there are limits to what a local church as a decision-making body should decide. Certain topics are out of bounds, off-limits, category errors. No local church has license

---

[2]Keith Mathison, *The Shape of Sola Scriptura* (Moscow, ID: Canon Press, 2001).

to redefine the historic Christian faith. Some doctrines are simply not open for debate. Each *ekklésia* is to operate within the bounds of orthodoxy. The elders are to rule off-limits the consideration of harmful and heretical ideas (1Ti 1:3). This is because the church at large today, and throughout time past, already has consensus on certain fundamental interpretations of Scripture. The Holy Spirit has not failed in His mission of guiding the church into all truth (Jn 16:13). As G. K. Chesterton said, "Tradition means giving votes to the most obscure of all classes, our ancestors. It is the democracy of the dead. Tradition refuses to submit to the small and arrogant oligarchy of those who merely happen to be walking about."[3]

Plural Leadership: New Testament references to local church leaders are generally in the plural. For instance: "they had appointed elders for them in every church" (Acts 14:23); "call for the elders of the church" (Ja 5:14). From such texts as these, many have inferred that each local church should, ideally, have a plurality of elders. Generally speaking, each church should have as many men serve as elders as are qualified. Ideally, it should be a plurality.[4] Some of the benefits of plural leadership are:

1. There is less chance of a dictatorship developing. Remember Lord Acton's wise words: "Power tends to corrupt, and absolute power corrupts absolutely. Great men are almost always bad men." However, even if there is only one brother qualified to serve as elder, an understanding that elder rule is to include building consensus among all the brothers will help avoid the development of a modern Diotrephes: "I have written something to the church, but Diotrephes, who likes to put himself first, does not acknowledge our authority. So if I come, I will bring up what he is doing, talking wicked nonsense against us. And not content with that, he refuses to welcome the brothers, and also stops those who want to and puts them out of the church" (3Jn 1:9-10).

[3] "Tradition Is the Democracy of the Dead," Chesterton.org, accessed September 1, 2016.

[4] As to the difference between an elder, overseer ("bishop" in the KJV), and pastor (shepherd), an examination of Acts 20:17, 28-30, Titus 1:5-7, and 1 Peter 5:1-3 will show the synonymous usage of these words. All three refer to the same leadership role.

2. There is a better advantage in dealing with an attack of wolves: "I know that after my departure fierce wolves will come in among you, not sparing the flock; and from among your own selves will arise men speaking twisted things, to draw away the disciples after them" (Acts 20:29-30). As Ecclesiastes says, "Though one may be overpowered, two can defend themselves. A cord of three strands is not quickly broken" (4:12).

3. There is greater wisdom: "By wise guidance you can wage your war, and in abundance of counselors there is victory" (Pr 24:6).

4. As reflected in Jethro's advice to Moses (Ex 18:13-27), a plurality of elders distributes the workload for hospital visitation, teaching, counseling, dealing with problems, etc.

5. It taps into a broader range of spiritual gifts. Not all elders are equally gifted or motivated: "Let the elders who rule well be considered worthy of double honor, especially those who labor in preaching and teaching" (1 Ti 5:17).

6. It has been said that it is lonely at the top. Being a sole elder can be lonely and discouraging. A plurality of elders makes for mutual encouragement.

Servant Leadership: The Scriptures refer to church leaders as servants. This emphasizes the need for courageous, humble, servant leadership. Today, many would flock to a leadership conference, but how many would be interested in a servant's conference? Jesus always taught, loved and lived by example that the Good Shepherd lays down his life for the sheep.

Jesus has authority over the church and all creation. Yet, when Jesus humbled Himself and became a man, He came to earth as a servant (Php 2:5-8). Jesus said: "the Son of Man came not to be served but to serve" (Mt 20:28). Jesus taught: "whoever would be first among you must be your slave" (Mt 20:27). Leaders are to be great in service.

Hebrews 13:17 indicates the church is to yield to its leaders. However, Jesus' comments on leadership must be both the starting point and final reference for understanding an elder's authority. Contrasting the authority of secular leaders with that of church leaders, Jesus declared, "But not so with you."[5] Instead, Jesus said the church leader's authority seems to be that of a child and a waiter—precisely those in Roman society who had the least authority in the normal sense of the word. Certainly, a church leader has more wisdom and understanding than a child. Indeed, he should be among the wisest in the church. Doubtless, there is a high degree of hyperbole in Jesus' words; yet, the application to be gleaned is that rather than lording over the church, church leaders are to serve the church by humble example. This type of "authority" will not work in secular governments nor business, but only in a redeemed community.

Elder Rule & Congregational Consensus: Elders are to guide, model, persuade, teach, feed, counsel, protect, warn, advise, rebuke, and correct. After a process of persuading, the church is to yield to its elders in the Lord. However, it is helpful to properly assess the relationship that existed in the New Testament era between local elders and their churches. For instance, there is a surprising *lack* of emphasis on local church leaders in New Testament writings. Instead of writing directly to the leaders, the apostles wrote to entire churches. Notice their leadership style. They did not simply issue directives. They urged, persuaded, argued, and convinced whole congregations. This is how elders are also to relate to their congregations. Elders must be imminently good at persuading with the truth. This apostolic emphasis on entire churches, rather than on just the leadership of the churches, arises from the fact that responsibility for decision making rests with the *ekklésia* (church) as a whole together with its elders.[6]

---

[5]Luke 22:26.

[6]Notice how, in 1 Corinthians 5, Paul looked to the congregation as a whole to put out the man in sin. Paul did not instruct the elders to do it. This illustrates that ultimate authority lies with the congregation.

APPENDIX D

Strategically Small: Is your church small? If so, you have lots of company. Sixty percent of all Protestant churches in the U.S. have less than 100 adults attending.[1] Worldwide, over one *billion* Christians worship in churches of under 250 people.[2] This means small-church pastors shepherd over one billion of God's sheep.[3] First-century congregations were small too — gathering almost exclusively in private homes. It was these small churches that God used to turn the Roman world upside down.[4] Good things really do come in small packages! Small is part of a divine design. The small church strategies found in the New Testament can help make your small church of significance in God's kingdom.

Mega church pastor Adrian Rogers joked to those who preferred a smaller church, "Just sit in one of the first ten rows and don't look back!"[5] However, a genuine advantage small churches have is being positioned to reap strategic benefit from New Testament small church practice: participatory worship services, a weekly love feast (the *Agapé*), a plurality of elders who lead with the servant love of Christ, a commitment to congregational consensus and an understanding of the vital importance of making disciples by regularly teaching people to observe all that Jesus commanded.

According to the Barna Group's research, people un-der 35 are the most likely to consider attending a small church. Their stated desire is to be personally known and connected, something that can be more difficult to achieve in larger churches.[6] Small churches that follow the ways of the early church are in good position to offer what many

[1]"Small Churches Struggle to Grow Because of the People They Attract," Barna. org, accessed August 26, 2016.

[2]Karl Vaters, "The Astonishing Power of Small Churches: Over One Billion Served," ChristianityToday.com, accessed August 30, 2016.

[3]Vaters, ChristianityToday.com.

[4]Acts 17:6.

[5]Adrian Rogers, *Adrianisms* (Memphis, TN: Innovo Publishing 2015), 266.

[6]*Barna.org*

people are looking for: true fellowship, lasting and transparent relationships, and less politics.

Church Houses: Some Christians put entirely too much emphasis on church buildings. It is interesting that there is a total absence of any instruction in the New Testament regarding the construction of special buildings for worship. This is in contrast to Mosaic legislation, which contained very specific blueprints regarding the tabernacle. When the New Covenant writers did touch upon this subject, they pointed out that believers themselves are the temple of the Holy Spirit, living stones that come together to make up a spiritual house with Jesus Christ as the Chief Cornerstone (1Pe 2:4-5, Ep 2:19-22, 1Co 3:16, 6:19).

We should question when inordinate amounts of revenue are spent on purchasing and maintaining church buildings, revenue that could be better spent on disciple making, evangelism, benevolence and supporting workers. Objecting to the false veneration of buildings, Bernard of Clairvaux reportedly wrote: "I will not dwell upon the vast height of their churches, their unconscionable length, their preposterous breadth, their richly polished paneling ... Your candlesticks as tall as trees, great masses of bronze of exquisite workmanship, dazzling with their precious stones ... what, think you, is the purpose of all this? O vanity of vanities — no, insanity rather than vanities!"[7]

A church building is not a church—it's just a sheep shed. That's why Donald Guthrie concluded that "the expression 'in church' (*en ekklésia*) ... refers to an assembly of believers. There is no suggestion of a special building. Indeed, the idea of a church as representing a building is totally alien to the NT."[8] Believers themselves are the temple of the Holy Spirit, living stones who come together to make up a spiritual house with Jesus Christ as Chief Cornerstone.[9]

Itinerant English Bible teacher Arthur Wallis said, "In the Old Testament, God had a sanctuary for His people; in

---

[7]David Calhoun, Church History Course, Covenant Theological Seminary.
[8]Donald Guthrie, *New Testament Theology* (Downers Grove, IL: IVP, 1981), 744.
[9]1 Peter 2:4-5, Ephesians 2:19-22, 1 Corinthians 3:16, 6:19.

the New, God has His people as a sanctuary."[10] Consider the penetrating words of John Havlik: "The church is never a place, but always a people; never a fold but always a flock; never a sacred building but always a believing assembly. The church is you who pray, not where you pray. A structure of brick or marble can no more be the church than your clothes of serge or satin can be you. There is in this world ... no sanctuary of man but the soul."[11]

The churches in the New Testament met in private Roman villas. This practice continued until around the time Constantine legalized Christianity with the Edict of Milan in A.D. 313. After that, the construction of church buildings began in earnest. Pagan temples became huge Christian places of worship (such as happened with the Pantheon in Rome). Worst yet, Christians began to treat their new church buildings with the same reverence that the Hebrews had for the Jerusalem Temple. For example, there were no toilets in early church buildings. The thought seems to have been that such facilities were incompatible with the holy nature of the building.[12]

Charles Spurgeon asked, "Does God need a house? He who made the heavens and the earth, does he dwell in temples made with hands? What crass ignorance this is! No house beneath the sky is more holy than the place where a Christian lives, and eats, and drinks, and sleeps, and praises the Lord in all that he does, and there is no worship more heavenly than that which is presented by holy families, devoted to the fear of the Lord."[13] The real issue is, thus, not where a church meets, but where and how it can best do what God requires of it.

House Churches: Many forward thinkers suspect the church in the West is headed for a relationship with civil government similar to that already existing in China or Iran where the church has largely been driven underground. As

---

[10]Arthur Wallis, *The Radical Christian* (Rancho Cordova, CA: City Hill Publishing, 1987).

[11]John Havlik, *People Centered Evangelism* (Nashville: Broadman Publishers, 1971), 47.

[12]Peter Davids and Siegfried Grossmann, "The Church in the House," paper, 1982, footnote 22.

[13]Charles Spurgeon, sermon, "Building The Church," April 5, 1874.

secularized administrations continue to get elected in the West, church teachings against sexual immorality will be increasingly portrayed as intolerant hate speech. Christians will be painted by the godless media and atheist government as backwards, close-minded, religious bigots. It is proverbial that the power to tax is the power to destroy. The tax-exempt status of many churches and Christian schools will likely be revoked as government legislation prioritizes sexual freedom over religious rights. In times of persecution, meeting in private homes becomes an increasingly attractive option.

J. Vernon McGee predicted, "As the church started in the home, it is going to come back to the home."[14] Given the right circumstances, a private home can still be the ideal setting for a church meeting. The smaller, homey setting fosters genuine friendships. The Lord's Supper celebrated as a fellowship meal in this relaxed, unhurried, comfortable setting helps build unity and love. Since a home is not big enough to accommodate a huge number of people, participatory worship wherein each person contributes according to his spiritual gift is much more intimate and meaningful. Using suitable private dwellings where possible is a good use of scarce financial resources. Because every member's participation and ministry were highly valued and encouraged in the early church, a large home is still a good setting wherein every person can comfortably contribute and function for the edification of the whole body of Christ. House churches can be simple, wonderful, down-to-earth (yet touching heaven) expressions of new covenant church life.

The problem is that many modern homes are simply too small to hold enough believers to have the strength of a New Testament house church. Thus, in a typical, modern, Western house church, no one is qualified to serve as elder and no one gifted to teach. Lacking leadership, the house church becomes more of a "bless me" club. The fellowship is fantastic, the worship is wonderful, and the kids have a good time playing together. However, no significant discipleship takes place. Outreach is minimal. The congregation is so small there is

[14]J. Vernon McGee, *Thru the Bible: Philippians and Colossians* (Nashville: Thomas Nelson, 1991), 190.

no way a pastor or missionary could be supported. Even if the home is big enough to host a fair number of people, your neighbors will not be pleased if, every Lord's Day, the streets around your house are choked with cars.[15] Many counties have passed zoning ordinances against churches in homes for this very reason.

In all, to accomplish what the early church accomplished may necessitate *not* meeting in homes (but rather some dynamic equivalent).[16] Therefore the real emphasis should be on New Testament church practice in general, not simply meeting in homes. To function as effectively as the early church functioned, a church building's size and layout should be carefully considered. Ideally, it should have a homey feel, be designed to house a relatively small congregation and its seating arrangement flexible. Since eating together was a big part of early gatherings, it should have a food preparation area (sink, long counter top, refrigerator, etc.) and dining area. To help families with small children it should have a nursery and quality indoor and outdoor play areas. There should be ample parking.

Houston Baptist University professor Peter Davids and German Baptist pastor Siegfried Grossman wrote, "The witness of the New Testament is clear: the living space of the church was the house. We judge the church-historical development to be a step backward from relationship to religion. Today a new desire for a face-to-face fellowship has broken out. For too long we have exclusively seen the formal church services as the center of the church and neglected our concrete life together in houses. We cannot slavishly imitate what took place earlier, but we should be challenged anew by this foundational structure of the church as a network of house churches. We see the following concrete challenges:

The church needs face to face fellowship.

The church dare not bracket out daily life from the life of the church.

---

[15] An ideal home has inconspicuous and ample off-street parking or is located across from a school parking lot or closed business.

[16] Such as a restaurant, community room, apartment club house, small church building, etc.

The church needs structures through which the reality of concrete life can be encouraged.

The church must keep in balance the handing out of the word and the handing out of life."[17]

Small in a Big Way: Pastors deeply desire to see their churches grow both spiritually and numerically. They want to reach people with the Gospel and see lives transformed. A small church with the life of Christ that adopts early church practice likely will grow both spiritually and numerically. As people's needs are met, as people walk closer with Christ, they get excited and can't help but tell others about both Christ and His church. Growing churches love and loving churches grow.

As your small church grows, the temptation will be to allow it to get bigger and bigger. However, past a certain size, a church will begin to lose the small church advantage. Following the practices of the New Testament will become more and more difficult. It will become a victim of its own success! The solution is to intentionally keep the church relatively small through the multiplication of new small churches. Continually train up new leaders and send out your best people to start new congregations. The goal is dynamic small churches that start other dynamic small churches that start other dynamic small churches.

Celebrate the multiplication of small churches. Gauge success by multiplication rather than addition. Church growth consultant Bill Easum suggests, "Success shouldn't be measured solely by our worship attendance. Success must also be measured by how many people we send out and release into ministry."[18] There are 400,000 churches in America with an average size of 100.[19] If only 10% start a new church in the next five years, that would be 40,000 new churches. Now, that is something to get excited about!

---

[17]Davids & Grossmann.

[18]Bill Easum, "Ripples of Multiplication," m.exponential.org, accessed August 31, 2016.

[19]Bob Roberts, "Multiplication Essentials", m.exponential.org, accessed August 31, 2016.

The City Church Concept: It is entirely possible that New Testament house churches within a city were networked together, sharing elders and essentially functioning as one church though meeting in numerous locations. This approach can help overcome the limitations of modern Western homes being isolated and smaller than a Roman villa. The elders from the various house churches could meet weekly as a sort of presbytery. A mid-week centralized teaching open to all house church members could be offered by those elders especially inclined toward a teaching ministry. The house congregations could also all meet together on a regular basis (monthly?) in some large rented facility for worship and encouragement.

Bi-Vocational Pastors: Often when serving a small church, it is necessary to be bi-vocational—working at a secular job to support your family. Famous are Jesus' words that it is more blessed to give than to receive. Not so well known is the context of those words. Not found in any of the four Gospels, Jesus' words were quoted by Paul at a pastor's conference. Paul assumed most of them would earn their livings working at regular jobs like he did and, thus, be in the position of *giving* silver and gold to the church, rather than receiving such from it: "I coveted no one's silver or gold or apparel. You yourselves know that these hands ministered to my necessities and to those who were with me. In all things I have shown you that by working hard in this way we must help the weak and remember the words of the Lord Jesus, how he himself said, 'It is more blessed to give than to receive.'"[20]

Most pastors feel a great burden for serving and reaching out, almost like Jeremiah: "If I say, 'I will not mention him, or speak any more in his name,' there is in my heart as it were a burning fire shut up in my bones, and I am weary with holding it in, and I cannot."[21] This creates the type of tension expressed by a bi-vocational pastor, who wrote, "I leave home at 5:30 a.m. and return at 5:30 p.m. While I see the people around me as an open field for ministry so much of my time is consumed

[20]Acts 20:33-35.
[21]Jeremiah 20:9

in commercial activities that I feel like there is something beyond all this that pulls my mind to it perpetually."[22]

I too have felt this tension. For over twenty-five years, I led a church and worked selling electronics parts to radio stations. One thing I focused on was serving the various engineers at the stations, seeking to share Christ with them and treating them with value as men made in God's image. I found solace in Paul's example. He was God's premier evangelist, church planter and disciple maker. Yet God, in his sovereignty, felt it was a good use of Paul's time to make tents. You may be thinking that since Paul was single, without a family, he still had more time for ministry than a bi-vocational pastor with a family. However, there is more. God's divine wisdom also judged it would be better for Paul to spend much of his time in jail, totally unable to do the "Lord's work." However, if not for that time in jail, the church might not have the prison epistles Paul wrote. Our idea of the Lord's work and His idea may be two different things! No one knows, not even you, the work God is doing in your life to prepare you for whatever is next. The question remains: Are you where he has called you to serve? If not, look elsewhere. If so, what else can you do but remain faithful and stay in place?

No matter what, your family must come first before an outside ministry. The church will have many pastors over the years, but your children will only have one father. Don't let your ministry become an idol. As time is short, find a way to spend less time in sermon preparation. Perhaps cover a smaller amount of Scripture but really well and with good application. Maybe teach a shorter time, or in a different way with more discussion or allow time for questions and input from the brothers about the sermon. Of course, there will be resistance, but inform the church that change must come (such as increased financial support, in the way church meetings are conducted, of what is expected of you) or else you will have to step down. Roll your burden onto Him. It is His church anyway, not ours. Jesus promised to build the church. Let us rest in God's sovereignty.

---

[22]E-mail correspondence between author and a South African pastor.

APPENDIX E

Lifelessness: Jesus came that we might have life and have it abundantly.[1] Critical to any outworking of church life is first having an inner life to work out. Technically correct church practice without the wine of the Spirit is a hollow shell. It is dry, seasoned wood, all stacked up, with no fire. Jesus is the Vine and we are the branches. Apart from Jesus we can no nothing.[2] It is folly to give attention to outward perfection while neglecting that which is vital—a daily walk with the risen Lord. Jesus is the reality; apostolic church practice is the application of that reality.

License: A temptation for those who truly possess the inner reality of life in Jesus is to treat its outward expression as a matter of liberty. Having the greater (the wine), they feel that they themselves are competent to decide in lesser matters (the wineskin). They believe they have a license from the Spirit to do whatever they please with the outward form. To be bound by the ways of the apostles is seen as mindless mimicking. However, Jesus warned that pouring new wine into the wrong container could lead to the loss of the wine (Mt 9:17). Do we really know better than the apostles how to organize churches? Specifically with reference to church practice, Paul admonished, "If anyone thinks that he is a prophet, or spiritual, he should acknowledge that the things I am writing to you are a command of the Lord" (1Co 14:37).

Legalism: Beware of making patterns out of silence. Some are convinced that we should follow New Testament patterns, but further that we have no freedom to do anything that was not done by the early church. They believe that if a practice is not found in the New Testament, then we can't do it; it is forbidden. For instance, if the New Testament is silent about using musical instruments, then they must not be used. This is known as the regulative principle. In response, it must first be pointed out that the lack of mention of a practice is not proof

---

[1] John 10:10.
[2] John 15:5.

the early church did not practice it. Second, this negative approach is essentially a form of legalism and leads easily to a judgmental spirit. Instead of seeking to positively follow clear New Testament patterns, advocates of this negative hermeneutic are best known for all the things they are against. Finally, if the regulative principle is the right approach, then why did Jesus participate in the festival of Hanukkah and synagogue system, both of which were extra-biblical, inter-testament historical developments?

The Roman world is gone forever. There is a big difference between holding to apostolic tradition versus mindlessly copying *everything* seen in the New Testament (wearing sandals and togas, writing on parchment, reading by oil lamps, etc.). The key is to focus on New Testament church practice. We must also beware of making patterns out of things that are not patterns in the New Testament. For instance, the Christian communalism of Acts 4 was a onetime event for a single church. It is an option for believers of any age, but it is neither a command nor a Scriptural pattern.

Liberty: Instead of the regulative principle, adopt a normal hermeneutic that insists the church normally holds to those practices clearly followed by the early church. Matters of silence are matters of freedom. If the Bible is silent about something—if there is neither command nor pattern to follow—then we have the liberty to do whatever suits us (following the leading of the Holy Spirit).

Are there ever any good reasons for going against New Testament patterns? Moses told the Israelites to observe a Saturday Sabbath—violating it was a capital offense. However, if an ox was in the ditch, it was acceptable to work on the Sabbath. Jesus—the Lord of the Sabbath—clarified that it was also always appropriate to do good works on the Sabbath. He further taught how the Sabbath was made for man and not man for the Sabbath. So too, the examples found in the New Testament are there for the sake of the church, not *vice versa*. Scripture indicates we are generally to keep the patterns laid down by the apostles. However, there are times when there will be extenuating circumstances that argue against keeping some of the patterns. Just don't let the exception become the rule.

BIBLIOGRAPHY

Aristotle, *Aristotle's Rhetoric*, Book I, chapter 2.

Banks, Robert, *Paul's Idea of Community: The Early House Churches in Their Historical Setting*, Grand Rapids: Eerdmans, 1988.

Barclay, William, *The Letters to the Corinthians*, Philadelphia: Westminster, 1977.

Barrett, C. K., *The Fist Epistle to the Corinthians*, *Black's New Testament Commentary*, Peabody: Hendrickson, 1968.

Bauer, Arndt, Gingrich, Danker, *A Greek-English Lexicon of the New Testament*, Chicago: University of Chicago Press, 1979.

Belgic Confession, Article 29.

Broadbent, E.H., *The Pilgrim Church*, Grand Rapids: Gospel Folio Press 1999.

Brown, Colin, *New International Dictionary of New Testament Theology*, Vol. III, Grand Rapids: Zondervan, 1981.

Bruce, F.F., *Acts of The Apostles*, Grand Rapids, MI: Eerdmans, 1981.

Calhoun, David, Church History Course, Covenant Theological Seminary.

Chesterton, G.K., "Tradition Is the Democracy of the Dead," Chesterton.org.

Coenen, Lothan, "Church," ed., Brown, Colin, *The New International Dictionary of New Testament Theology*, Grand Rapids: Zondervan, 1971.

Dagg, J.L., *Manual of Theology: A Treatise on Church Order*, Harrisonburg, VA: Gano Books, 1990.

Davids, Peter and Grossmann, Siegfried, "The Church in the House," paper, 1982.

Deddens, Karl, *Where Everything Points to Him*, translated by Theodore Plantinga, Neerlandia, Alberta: Inheritance Publications, 1993.

Dennis, Lane, ed. *ESV Study Bible*, Wheaton: Crossway, 2008.

DeVries, David, "How Much Does It Cost To Start A Church?", MissionalChallenge.com.

Drane, John, *Introducing the New Testament*, Oxford: Lion, 1999.

Elliot, Elizabeth, *Shadow of The Almighty: Life and Testimony of Jim Elliot*, San Francisco: Harper & Row, 1989.

Fee, Gordon & Stuart, Douglas, *How To Read The Bible For All Its Worth*, 1st ed., Grand Rapids: Zondervan, 1982.

Fee, Gordon, *New International Commentary on the New Testament, The First Epistle to The Corinthians*, Grand Rapids: Eerdmans, 1987.

Gaustad, Edwin, *Liberty of Conscience: Roger Williams In America*, Grand Rapids: Eerdmans, 1991.

Godet, Frederick, *Commentary on Luke*, Grand Rapids: Kregel 1981.

Greensdale, Stanley Lawrence, "Early Christian Church," *Encyclopaedia Britannica*, Vol. 7, ed. Warren Preece, Chicago: William Benton, Publisher, 1973.

Grogan, G. W., "Love Feast," *The New Bible Dictionary*, ed., J. D. Douglas, Wheaton: Tyndale, 1982.

Grudem, Wayne, "The Nature of Divine Eternity, A Response to William Craig", WayneGrudem.com.

Guthrie, Donald, *New Testament Theology*, Downers Grove: Inter-Varsity, 1981.

Havlik, John, *People Centered Evangelism*, Nashville: Broadman, 1971.

Hendriksen, William *New Testament Commentary on Romans*, Grand Rapids: Baker, 1980.

Jeremias, Joachim, *The Eucharistic Words of Jesus*, New York: Charles Scribner's Sons, 1966.

John Gooch, *Christian History & Biography*, Issue 37, Carol Stream: Christianity Today.

Kirby, G.W., *Zondervan Pictorial Encyclopedia of the Bible*, Vol. 1, Grand Rapids: Zondervan 1982.

Koyzis, David, "The Lord's Supper: How Often?", ReformedWorship.org.

Lenski, R.C.H., *The Interpretation of I and II Corinthians*, Minneapolis: Augsburg, 1943.

Martin, R. P., "The Lord's Supper," *The New Bible Dictionary*, ed. J. D. Douglas, Wheaton: Tyndale, 1982.

Mathison, Keith, *The Shape of Sola Scriptura*, Moscow, Idaho: Canon Press, 2001.

McGee, J. Vernon, *Thru the Bible: Philippians and Colossians*, Nashville: Thomas Nelson, 1991.

McReynolds, Paul, *Word Study Greek-English New Testament*, Wheaton: Tyndale, 1999.

Milikin, Jimmy, "Disorder Concerning Public Worship," *Mid America Baptist Theological Journal*, Memphis: Mid-America Baptist Seminary Press, 1983.

Murphy-O'Connor, Jerome, *Saint Paul's Corinth: Texts and Archaeology* (Collegeville, MN: Liturgical Press, 2002),

Nee, Watchman, *The Normal Christian Church Life*, Colorado Springs: International Students Press, 1969.

Pelikan, Jaroslav, "Eucharist," *Encyclopaedia Britannica*, ed. Warren Preece, Vol. 8, Chicago: William Benton, Publisher, 1973.

Price, Charles, Director of Missions, San Antonio Baptist Association, personal conversation.

Reinecker, Fritz & Rogers, Cleon, *Linguistic Key to the Greek New Testament*, Grand Rapids: Zondervan, 1980.

Ridderbos, Herman, *Paul: An Outline of His Theology*, translated by John R. deWitt, Grand Rapids: Eerdmans, 1975.

Robertson & Plummer, *International Critical Commentary on the Holy Scriptures of the Old and New Testaments, 1 Corinthians*, New York: Charles Scribner's Sons, 1911.

Rogers, Adrian, *Adrianisms* (Memphis, TN: Innovo Publishing 2015.

Scott, Ernest, *The Nature Of The Early Church*, New York, Charles Scribner's Sons, 1941.

Sefton, Henry, *A Lion Handbook - The History of Christianity*, Oxford: Lion, 1988.

Sider, Ronald, *Rich Christians in an Age of Hunger*, Downers Grove, IL: InterVarsity, 1977.

"Small Churches Struggle to Grow Because of the People They Attract," Barna.org.

Smith, William, *A Dictionary of Greek and Roman Antiquities*, London: John Murray, 1875.

Snyder, James, *Tozer On Worship And Entertainment*, Camp Hill, PA: Wind Hill Publisher, 1997.

Spurgeon, Charles, sermon, "Building The Church."

Synder, Graydon, *Church Life Before Constantine*, Macon, GA: Mercer University Press, 1991.

Thayer, Joseph, *Greek-English Lexicon of the New Testament*, Grand Rapids: Baker, 1977.

Theissen, Gerd, *The Social Setting of Pauline Christianity: Essays on Corinth*, Eugene, OR: Wipf & Stock, 1982.

Thomas, W.H. Griffith, *St. Paul's Epistle to the Romans*, Grand Rapids: Eerdmans, 1984.

"Unearthing the Christian Building", *Dura-Europos: Excavating Antiquity*, Yale University Art Gallery.

Vaters, Karl, "The Astonishing Power of Small Churches: Over One Billion Served," ChristianityToday.com.

Vine, W.E., *Expository Dictionary of New Testament Words*, Iowa Falls: Riverside Book and Bible House, 1952.

Wallis, Arthur, *The Radical Christian*, Rancho Cordova, CA: City Hill Publishing, 1987.

Watson, David, *I Believe in the Church*, Great Britain: Hodder & Stoughton, 1978.

"Why Do Newly Planted Churches Grow Faster Than Older Churches?", rmdc.org.

1599 Geneva Bible, White Hall, West Virginia: Telle Lege Press, 2006.

2000 Baptist Faith and Message, sbc.net.

ABOUT THE AUTHOR

Stephen Atkerson serves as an elder in the Southern Baptist church he helped plant in 1991. Since its inception the church has been blessed by following early church practice. Other distinctives of the church include an emphasis on new covenant theology and complementarian roles for men and women. His favorite statement of faith is the First London Baptist Confession of 1644. Married 34 years before his wife went to be with the Lord, he has three grown children and four grandchildren.

Stephen has been involved with churches that range in size from the very largest to the very smallest. He was baptized under the ministry of Charles Stanley at First Baptist Atlanta and then later served as director of the college department at First Baptist Birmingham. During his time at Mid-America Baptist Seminary in Memphis, he participated in the internship program at Bellevue Baptist (Adrian Rogers, pastor). Stephen then served seven years on the pastoral staff of a mid-sized Southern Baptist church in Atlanta. In the late 80s, he began working with small churches that followed the four practices detailed in this book.

He is president of the New Testament Reformation Fellowship (NTRF.org), a ministry focused on reforming today's church with New Testament church practice. Through NTRF he has worked with church leaders throughout the United States and in Canada, South America, China, New Zealand, England, Germany, Switzerland, Russia, India, and Sri Lanka.

About NTRF

The Protestant Reformation of the 1500s began a reform of church practice and belief. As wonderful as the Reformation was, the Magisterial Reformers stopped short of fully reforming church practice. The Baptists of the 1600s took reform a step further, insisting on the separation of church and state, believer's baptism and the autonomy of each local church. The New Testament Reformation Fellowship is simply a fellowship of brothers who desire to continue the reformation of today's church by the adoption of New Testament church practice.

NTRF's mission is to provide resources and training in how the early church met together in community. We seek to aid others in recapturing the intimacy, simplicity, accountability and dynamic of Spirit-led first century church life. God has opened doors of opportunity for us to present these concepts to believers in North and South America, Europe, Asia, and Oceania.

We argue from Scripture for such things as first-century Roman-villa-sized churches, the Lord's Supper as fellowship feast (a sacred, covenant meal), participatory worship services, and elders who are truly servant leaders and not lords (government by elder-led congregational consensus). Our goal is to be Christ-honoring and thoroughly biblical in every area of church life.

The essential tenets of the faith to which we subscribe are identical to those found in the doctrinal statements of any sound evangelical institution. Our favorite statement of faith is the First London Baptist Confession of 1644. In particular, those of us associated with NTRF agree with the doctrines of grace, new covenant theology, the 1978 Chicago Statement on Biblical Inerrancy, the 1987 Danvers Statement, and the 2017 Nashville Statement.

GOOD NEWS

I jokingly tell people I had a drug problem growing up because my parents drug me to church! Though I had heard of Jesus since my earliest memory, my belief in him was not unlike my belief in Albert Einstein: I was not against him but neither did I look to him to do anything for me. Mistakenly I thought heaven my destiny simply because I sincerely tried to be a good person.

In my freshman year of high school my mother passed away from cancer. My concern was what had become of her. Where had she gone? Would I ever see her again? After much inquiry about life after death, I discovered that eternal life is not based on our own goodness, but the goodness of Jesus. No matter how good I was it could not be good enough. God is so holy that just one sin is all it takes to separate us from him. That was bad news. The good news is that Jesus, who is God in human form, died on the cross in order to pay for sin. Since He is infinite God, Jesus was able suffer in a finite amount of time on the cross what it would take me, who am finite, an infinity of time to suffer in hell. After dying and being buried, Jesus literally, bodily rose from the dead on the third day. He conquered death! He then ascended to heaven and from there Christians await his return.

When I realized the truth, I consciously transferred trust for my eternal destiny from me and anything good in me over to Jesus. I confessed the same thing that Thomas, an early believer, confessed: "My Lord and my God!" (John 20:28). After trusting in Jesus he gave me the desire to learn about and obey His teachings. As he himself said, "If you love me, you will keep my commandments" (John 14:15).

My appeal is that you look to Jesus for eternal life. Worship him as your Lord and God. Call on Him while He is near. Behold! Now is the day of salvation. To learn more, find the Gospel of John in the Bible. Read it a chapter at a time. At the end of each chapter ask yourself two questions, based on that chapter: 1) Who is Jesus? 2) What does he want from me? There are 21 chapters in John's Gospel. Will you accept the 21-Day Challenge and read a chapter a day?

"A fresh breath of theological insight to me when I was desperately seeking God with the prayer, 'Lord, there has to be more about your church. Help me discover it.'"

REUBEN P.
Indigenous Indian missionary; pastor

"The Lord began to reveal to me what his church should be like. The information in this book became my foundation. It very accurately and thoroughly details all the legacies left to us by the apostles of Jesus Christ. They left a pattern for us to build a church, such as it should be. The individual pieces of my understanding of the church this material folded into the whole picture."

ANDREY MIKLIN
Indigenous Russian church planter; pastor

"A great practical tool for pastors, church planters, missionaries, and all Christians seeking to live out basic cross-cultural New Testament Church principles in local churches today."

JOSHUA B.
U.S. missionary; Asia

"Good practical ecclesiology. Applying these things can bring joy and growth to the assembly. May this book be a blessing to many!"

A.P.
Indigenous Asian church planter

"There is much here to help you think through how to recover vibrant church life, even if you see it differently here or there. Unmuddle your ecclesiastical grey matter by reading and contemplating these challenging principles."

JIM ELLIFF
President, Christian Communicators Worldwide

"The antidote to the evangelical obsession with the 'bigger is better' model of church organisation. It is not a cure-all panacea for the many ills in the church today; however it is the start of a conversation that may—with God's help—lead to much-needed reform. If you would like to know what church patterned after New Testament principles and practices looks like, then New Testament Church Dynamics is for you."

ROBERT MILLAR
Pastor, Bridge Church of Strabane, N. Ireland

"A compelling and thorough Biblical case for the modern church returning to some of the foundational practices of the early church with very practical steps to help the pastor institute these practices in today's church. With over 40 years of pastoral experience, I can truthfully say this book should be required reading for all church planters."

A.T. STEWART
Retired Southern Baptist pastor

"How can the church survive and even multiplied in nations where it experiences great intolerance and persecution? It's rather simple. Follow the proven practices and examples of the early church as set forth in God's word. In this short but thought-provoking work we have a survival guide."

MOE BERGERON
Teaching-elder, Sovereign Grace Fellowship, New Hampshire

"An ecclesiology rooted in New Testament church practice rather than in the shifting sands of contemporary church growth fads. After establishing normative church practice from NT church patterns, the author then gives pragmatic ways those practices can be implemented within modern western culture, thus happily integrating practice with theology. This book is a godsend for those frustrated by the failures of modern evangelical "models" for church practice, and for those who are discovering that the model provided by the Holy Spirit-inspired apostles is the most practical model of them all."

DAN TROTTER, *retired U.S. missionary to China*

"Built on sound exegesis and providing the documentation of scholars as backup, Steve Atkerson delivers a manual that is both scripturally compelling and practical . . . a must read for the church plant as well as established churches looking to leave the norms of dead traditionalism and return to the joy of the ekklesia of the New Testament."

CHRIS FALES
Church planter; founder, PorchCon New Covenant Theology Conferences

---

"In a day where 'How To' is rarely backed up with 'Why To', a work arrives where these thoughts meet. This timely resource is supported by timeless Biblical insights to assist those who seek to put into practice what many simply theorize about. Convincing, convicting, and illuminating, this handbook provides a glimpse into how church life was in the first century and how it can be in this century.

TIM ANDREWS
Pastor; church planter; USA